MW01679988

My Cottage Kitchen

COOKBOOK

Introduction

What makes a person want to cook so passionately? Is it an artistic expression in a different medium? I really don't know the answer to that question. However, I do know that for me it is a creative outlet and one that I feel compelled to express on a daily basis. It's not so much a desire but more like a need. I crave cooking just as others crave chocolate and different types of food. I often find myself day dreaming about recipes and their components and how to execute them. I contemplate menus and different combinations of meals. I study and collect cookbooks as many of you do. In fact I've been known to sit and read them like others read novels. However, more than anything I love to please those around me and most often I accomplish this with home cooked food. My family have their favorites of course and I know what they are, just like I know the back of my own hand. I also know my way around a kitchen and I can cook for two or forty-eight people without blinking an eye!

I'm a transplanted southerner that has generational roots in Mississippi and Louisiana; I was born in Virginia and raised in Tennessee. I'm very proud of my heritage as my family can tell you. I'm a true southern girl living in upstate New York. I have adored getting to know the area and learning its culture, heritage, people and food. I have adopted some of the cooking methods from the melting pot of this region but I have to be honest and tell you that my cooking will always reflect my southern upbringing and to me that is comfort in itself. You will see some of the southern dishes in this cookbook that have been some of my favorites for a very long time.

Our summers are spent in a cottage that is almost 100 years old and located on a lake in the very picturesque foothills of the Catskill Mountains in upstate New York. This cottage happens to proudly showcase my very favorite kitchen and to me its heaven on earth. Simply stated - I'm at peace in this kitchen. "My Cottage Kitchen" is so very special because of the wealth of wonderful family and friends that gather in that sacred room over food and drink made from loving recipes that have been passed down through generations and aspiring new ones. I like to think that people bond over food and lifetime memories are created each time we sit at the communal table together. Our summers are just a quick blur by the time September rolls around but we know how to squeeze absolutely the last minute of time left in the few short months of an ever fleeing New York season. We are experts at cramming a multitude of visiting guest into every available date! The time is passed by enjoying moonlit boat rides, blueberry picking, canoe rides, fishing, swimming, bon-fires, fireworks, tubing, paddle boarding, walking, tennis, hiking and just good quality time spent on the dock laughing and catching up with each other. We are the luckiest people on earth with the abounding love of friends, family and the truly scenic landscape of the countryside. Our good fortune is teamed with the beauty of rolling hills, mountains, rivers, creeks, waterfalls, dairy farms, corn farms, apple orchards and so much more. Our summers are coveted since our winters are long, cold, snowy and dark. We relish every precious moment between Memorial Day and Labor Day, and as beautiful as our autumn is, it comes very quickly!

My wish would be that you are grateful each time you share a meal with your family and friends, for your blessings are having a bountiful table and the fellowship of people that you love the most. I feel so truly thankful to be living in a free country with a beautiful family, great friends, an abundance of food and the ability to share my good fortune with others. May God bless each of you.

Your friend,
Tracy Maines

Table of Contents

A Very Special Message

Hunger in America

A few years ago my very dear friend Kathy and I discovered that we were both at a loss as to what to purchase for each other during the holiday season. After tossing thoughts back and forth it was evident that if we were struggling to come up with ideas for our gift exchange then obviously we needed absolutely nothing. However, with it being Christmas we just simply couldn't let it go at that. After careful consideration we decided that instead of buying something for each other we would do something meaningful for those less fortunate. Our decision of choosing to volunteer at a local food pantry hit a sweet spot for both of us and shortly thereafter we visited one in our area. We knew immediately we were in the right place as it hit all the bells and whistles we were looking for in a volunteering endeavor. I must tell you that it has been the gift that keeps on giving. I think we both receive so much more in return than we could ever possibly give.

It has been a gratifying education and humbling experience. I have learned so much about hunger in our community and I believe that this dire situation does not have to exist in our area or much less in our country. One of the many misconceptions about hunger in America is that people aren't able to provide food for themselves or their family because they aren't willing to work, in the vast majority of cases this is simply not true. Actually it can be the exact opposite as many of our clients do hold jobs and sometimes ambitiously more than one. While some clients hold common denominators as to why they need food assistance, others have very unique circumstances.

Hunger can hide behind many different faces, one of them being an elderly woman that looks just like your grandmother, which whom simply cannot work and survives off of her meager Social Security income. She is torn between choosing food or medication and sometimes receiving neither is the sad truth because she has to pay her heating bill instead. I have seen United States Military Veterans stand in line for food because they aren't able to work, perhaps due to a physical or mental disability. They may struggle gaining employment once they are out of the service for a multitude of reasons. It very well could be a middle aged woman who has been laid off of her job and because she is close to retirement age she may not be a desirable candidate for many employers. It's not for lack of trying, as some of the clients actually might accept the only job offered which is part-time work at a big box store; but there are no health benefits available, it only pays minimum wage and that simply doesn't pay the bills. There are the families with multiple children and the parents are working, but they aren't making an adequate income to make ends meet. It is truly sad to think that a child is deprived of eating three meals a day because school is not in session due to it being a weekend, a snow day or summer break. Once these children are back at school they are much more food secure in knowing that they will receive breakfast and lunch on the school free or reduced price meal program and a food pantry may be suppling the evening meal. I think of the single mothers who will feed their children first tonight and if there is anything left she may be able to eat, if not she will sleep on an empty stomach. Can you imagine yourself explaining to a child that they can't eat because there is no food? How do you explain the denial of a basic human need?

It is a fact that 1 in 6 people in America are food insecure. Hunger has no boundaries and it happens consistently throughout the year. The waiting line for clients starts hours ahead of the doors opening in the harsh elements of heat, rain, ice and snow. It is not a convenient drill for those who are hungry, as they will wait all day for a box of food all the while in very poor conditions. Hunger knows no gender, race, religion or age. Hunger can be a very indiscriminate and perpetual annoying monkey on your back that is hard to overcome. You never know when you pass someone on the street if they may have visited a food pantry or a soup kitchen recently. It could be your neighbor, co-worker, fellow student, the person sitting beside you at the ball park or on a church pew. It's worth noting that hunger is really a side effect of many different issues. The list of culprits that actually cause hunger is pages long, whether it be from physical illness, mental illness, old age, economic problems, drug addiction, alcoholism, unemployment or the death of a family member which whom may have been the main bread winner. Some situations are temporary until one can get on their feet, others can be more long term. At the end of the day it doesn't really matter why people visit a food pantry, as it's not our place to judge. We are only there for the soul purpose of assisting our fellow man. We are all equally susceptible to the harsh realities of a poor and struggling economy and ever changing social issues.

Let us all help conquer this multi-layered national issue by lending a hand. I encourage you to give of your time by starting a fundraiser, honor someone's birthday, memorialize a loved one, challenge your co-workers, match donations or simply give a monetary contribution to a local organization that feeds the hungry. There are many soup kitchens, pantries, church organizations and food banks in your area that would welcome your assistance! Lastly; be grateful for the food set forth in front of you each day, share with others, be aware of the food that you allow to go to waste and count each loaf of bread as if it were gold.

IT IS WITH GRATEFULNESS IN MY HEART THAT I PLEDGE TO DONATE ANY PROFITS OR CONTRIBUTIONS FROM THIS COOKBOOK TO A LOCAL FOOD BANK, FOOD PANTRY, SOUP KITCHEN OR ANY ORGANIZATION THAT PROVIDES ASSISTANCE TO THE HUNGRY.

A Well Stocked Pantry

A Well Organized and Stocked Pantry

In my world there is nothing more annoying than to start preparing a meal and midstream find that you don't have all of the ingredients to finish it. That drives me right over the edge! I like to think that one of my better attributes is my organizational skills and I sleep better at night knowing that. Our household can be a wee bit hectic to say the least, so having everything at hand is reassuring. We also don't have the privilege of a grocery store being located just around the corner as it's a bit of a drive over the river and through the woods, so it's all the better if I stay one step ahead.

I feel comforted in knowing that my pantry is stocked and I can make almost anything at a moments notice. If company drops by I have many of the makings at my fingertips to whip something together. I have compiled a list of all the ingredients that I have used in this cookbook into several categories which are on the following pages. Obviously you wouldn't buy all of the perishable items at once but at least having all of the non-perishable items on hand is a good start. It's also a lifesaver when it comes to taking some of the burden off of you're weekly trips to the market. I understand each household is different in their personal taste and preferences, but perhaps it will encourage you to stop and take note of which items you purchase on a regular basis...and you too can personalize your own list. I must add that it actually helps to be familiar with what's in your cupboard in order to take advantage of procuring needed items once they are on sale.

My pantry is organized with all like things together so it is easy to inventory what I'm missing and what I need to purchase at a quick glance. It's also more efficient when other people are pitching in as they can find items quickly for themselves. All of the soups are logically with the other soups, all of the canned tomatoes are with the canned tomatoes and all of the pasta is with the pasta and so on and so on. Keep your labels showing and rotate your products so you can use older and soon to be expired items first.

I believe being organized saves so much costly and precious time. After you have worked all day or have been away from home after a long day of errands you can easily prepare a home cooked meal by having everything right at your fingertips. Being in the kitchen should be fun and not feel like a chore. Do your best to make it uncomplicated and as enjoyable as possible for yourself, your family and your friends...I think your food will taste better too!

Happy Cooking!

Dried Herbs, Fresh Herbs and Spices

DRIED HERBS AND SPICES
Allspice
Basil
Bay Leaves
Celery Salt
Celery Seed
Chili Powder
Cinnamon, Ground
Cinnamon, Sticks
Cloves, Ground
Coriander, Ground
Cumin
Curry Powder
Garlic Powder
Garlic Salt
Italian Seasoning
Mint, Dried
Mustard, Coleman's Dry
Nutmeg, Ground
Nutmeg, Whole
Old Bay Seasoning
Onion Powder

Oregano
Paprika
Parsley
Pimiento Seeds (Jamaican Allspice)
Pepper, Ground Black
Pepper, Ground Cayenne
Pepper, Ground Whole
Pepper, Crushed Red
Pepper, Lemon
Peppercorns, Whole Black
Poultry Seasoning
Rosemary
Sage
Salt, Iodized Table
Salt, Kosher
Salt, Sea
Season All
Thyme

FRESH HERBS
Basil
Chervil
Chives
Cilantro
Dill
Marjoram
Mint
Oregano
Parsley
Rosemary
Tarragon
Thyme
Sage

Fresh Produce

Apples (Cortland, Jonathan, Golden Delicious or Granny Smith)
Arugula
Asparagus
Avocados
Bananas
Beets
Blackberries
Blueberries
Broccoli
Brussel Sprouts
Cabbage
Carrots
Celery
Chives
Collard Greens
Corn
Cranberries
Cucumber
Garlic
Ginger
Grapes, Seedless
Green Beans

Kale
Leeks
Lemons
Lettuce, Iceberg
Lettuce, Romaine
Limes
Mushrooms, Shiitake, Baby Bella, Cremini or Oyster
Onions, Green
Onions, Red
Onions, White
Onions, Yellow
Oranges, Navel
Peas, Sugar Snap
Peaches
Pears
Peppers, Habanero
Peppers, Jalapeño
Peppers, Scotch Bonnet
Peppers, Sweet Green Bell
Peppers, Sweet Red Bell
Peppers, Sweet Yellow Bell
Peppers, Thai Chile
Plantains
Potatoes, Red New
Potatoes, Russet
Potatoes, Sweet
Potatoes, Yukon Gold
Raspberries
Shallots
Spinach
Spinach, Baby
Squash, Summer
Strawberries
Tomatoes, Cherry
Tomatoes, Grape
Tomatoes, Green
Tomatoes, Red (Assorted Varieties)
Watermelon
Zucchini

Meats and Seafood

MEATS
Bacon
Bacon, Canadian
Beef Chuck Roast, Boneless
Beef Ground Chuck, 80/20 mix
Beef Ground Sirloin, 85/15 mix
Beef Ground Sirloin, Lean
Beef Prime Rib Roast
Beef Rump Roast
Beef Shanks
Beef Stew Meat, Cubed
Beef Tenderloin
Chicken Breast, Skinless
Chicken, Rotissierie
Chicken Tenders
Chicken Thighs, Boneless and Skinless
Chicken, Whole
Ham Bone

Ham, Deli Sliced Thin
Ham, Spiral Sliced Bone In
Lamb Chops
Lamb Shoulder
Lamb Tenderloin
Pancetta
Pepperoni
Pig Casings
Pork Chops, Thick Cut
Pork, Ground
Pork Tenderloin
Prosciutto
Salami
Sausage, Andouille
Sausage, Chorizo
Sausage, Italian Hot
Sausage, Italian Sweet
Sausage, Kielbasa
Turkey, Ground
Veal, Cutlets
Veal, Ground

SEAFOOD
Anchovy Paste
Clams, Small Littlenecks
Conch
Crab Meat, Lump
Salmon, Fillets
Shrimp, Large Uncooked 31/35, Peeled and Deveined
Shrimp, Small Frozen Cooked 150/250, Peeled and Deveined
Tilapia Fillets

Non-Perishable Pantry Items

ALCOHOL AND BEVERAGES
Beer (not light)
Coca-Cola
Coffee
Coffee, Instant
Cream De Cocoa
Rum, Appleton Estate
Whiskey, Jack Daniels
Wine, Red (i.e. Cabernet)
Wine, Dry White (i.e. Chardonnay)

BAKING
Baking Powder
Baking Soda
Bisquick Baking Mix
Chips, Butterscotch
Chips, Peanut Butter
Chips, Semi Sweet Dark Chocolate
Chips, Sweetened Milk Chocolate
Chocolate Baking Squares, Unsweetened
Coco Lopez (Cream of Coconut)
Cocoa Powder
Coconut Flakes
Corn Meal, Yellow
Cornstarch
Cream of Tartar
Extract, Coconut
Extract, Vanilla
Flour, All Purpose
Flour, Whole Wheat
Marshmallows, Large
Marshmallows, Miniature
Milk, Condensed
Milk, Evaporated
Pie Crust, Prepared Graham Cracker
Pudding, Vanilla (Cook and Serve)
Sugar, Confectioner's
Sugar, Dark Brown
Sugar, Light Brown
Sugar, White

Yeast, Dry

CANDY
Candy Bar, Dark or Milk Chocolate
Heath Toffee Bars
M&M's

CANNED AND JARRED FOODS
Artichoke Hearts, Marinated
Beans, Baked
Beans, Black
Beans, Cannellini
Beans, Red Kidney
Beans, Refried
Beef, Dried
Corn, Creamed
Peppers, Chipotle in Adobo Sauce
Tomato, Paste
Tomato, Sauce
Tomatoes, Chopped
Tomatoes, Crushed
Tomatoes, Diced
Tomatoes, Pureed
Tomatoes, Sun Dried and Packed in Oil
Tomatoes, Rotel
Tuna, All White Packed in Water
Water Chestnuts

CANNED, DRIED AND JARRED FRUITS
Apple Rings, Candied
Applesauce
Cherries, Dried
Cherries, Maraschino
Cranberries, Dried
Fruit Cocktail
Mint Jelly
Pineapple, Chunks
Pineapple, Crushed
Pumpkin
Raisins

CEREALS AND GRAINS
Barley
Chia Seeds
Flaxseed, Ground
Granola
Grits
Oatmeal, Quick Cooking
Polenta
Quinoa
Wheat Germ

CONDIMENTS
Capers, Pickled
Equal Sweetener
Horseradish, Prepared
Italian Dressing
Ketchup
Mayonnaise
Mustard, Creole
Mustard, Dijon
Mustard, Country Dijon
Mustard, Whole Grain Dijon
Mustard, Yellow
Olives, Black
Olives, Marinated Kalamata
Peperoncini, Pickled
Peppers, Pickled Banana
Peppers, Pickled Jalapeno
Pickles, Dill
Pickles, Sweet Relish
Pimientos
Sauce, Barbecue
Sauce, Jamaican Picka Pepper Sauce
Sauce, Soy
Sauce, Tabasco
Sauce, Taco (Medium or Hot)
Worcestershire Sauce

COOKIES AND CRACKERS
Cookies, Chocolate Sandwich
Cookies, Vanilla Wafers
Crackers, Graham
Crackers, Saltines

COOKING SUPPLIES
Aluminum Foil
Canning Jars, 8 ounce
Canning Jars, 12 ounce
Cooking Twine
Disposable Aluminum Pans, Half Size
Disposable Aluminum Pans, Full Size
Parchment Paper
Plastic Storage Wrap

DRY BEANS
Beans, Black
Beans, Red Kidney

NUTS
Almonds
Pecans
Pine Nuts
Walnuts, Chopped
Walnuts, Glazed

OILS AND FATS
Cooking Spray
Oil, Canola
Oil, Extra Virgin Olive
Oil, Vegetable
Shortening

PASTA AND RICE

Egg Noodles, Broad
Egg Noodles, Fine
Elbow Macaroni
Lasagna Noodles
Penne
Spaghetti
Wagon Wheel Pasta, Mini
White Rice, Long Grain
White Rice, Instant

SOUPS AND STOCKS

Bouillon Cubes, Beef
Soup, Tomato
Soup Mix, Onion
Soup Mix, Vegetable
Stock, Beef
Stock, Chicken

SPREADS AND SWEET TOPPINGS

Honey
Maple Syrup, Pure
Molasses
Peanut Butter

VINEGARS

Vinegar, Apple Cider
Vinegar, Balsamic
Vinegar, Balsamic Glaze
Vinegar, Champagne
Vinegar, Red Wine
Vinegar, Tarragon
Vinegar, White
Vinegar, White Wine

Perishable Pantry Items

BAKERY AND BREAD PRODUCTS
Bread, Ciabatta
Bread, Cinnamon Raisin
Bread, French Baguette
Bread, Italian
Bread, Pita
Bread, Sour Dough
Bread, White
Bread, White Country
Bread Crumbs, Panko
Bread Crumbs, Seasoned
Bread Crumbs, Unseasoned
Cake, Angel Food
Cake, Pound
Herb Stuffing Mix, Cubed
Tortilla, Chips
Tortillas, Corn
Tortillas, Flour

DAIRY, EGGS AND REFRIGERATOR ITEMS
Butter, Clarified (see directions under recipe "Brown Butter Sauce" in section "Sauces and Seasonings")
Butter, Salted
Butter, Unsalted
Buttermilk
Cream
Eggs
Half and Half
Heavy Cream
Heavy Whipping Cream
Garlic, Minced In Olive Oil
Guacamole, Prepared
Milk, Whole
Orange Juice
Pie Crust, Prepared
Sour Cream
Whipped Topping
Yogurt, Greek Plain

CHEESE
Cheese, Blue (Maytag)
Cheese, Cheddar (Extra Sharp)
Cheese, Cheddar (Mild)
Cheese, Cheddar (Sharp)
Cheese, Chèvre
Cheese, Cottage (Small Curd)
Cheese, Cream
Cheese, Feta
Cheese, Fontina
Cheese, Gruyere
Cheese, Monterey Jack
Cheese, Mozzarella
Cheese, Parmesan
Cheese, Parmigiano-Reggiano
Cheese, Pecorino Romano
Cheese, Queso Quesadilla
Cheese, Swiss

FROZEN
Beans, Green
Beans, Lima
Corn
Ice Cream, Vanilla
Peas, Green English
Spinach, Chopped
Tomatoes, Roasted (see recipe in section "Side Dishes")
Vegetables, Mixed

Appetizers

Beef Carpaccio

3 tablespoons black pepper, coarsely ground
2 tablespoons salt
2 tablespoons fresh thyme, finely chopped
3 tablespoons fresh marjoram, finely chopped
1 tablespoon garlic powder
1 pound beef tenderloin
1/4 cup olive oil
1 bunch arugula
Zippy Mayonnaise (see recipe in section "Sauces and Seasonings")
1/4 cup Parmesan cheese, grated
3 tablespoons parsley, chopped

Combine the black pepper, salt, thyme, marjoram and garlic powder in a shallow dish. Dry the tenderloin very well with paper towels. Lightly roll the tenderloin in the seasoning mix until all sides are evenly coated.

Add the olive oil to a medium size skillet and heat over medium high heat until hot. Sear the seasoned tenderloin on all sides for 1 minute. Do not overcook. You are looking for caramelization on the outside of the tenderloin and a very rare temperature on the inside. Remove the tenderloin from the skillet and cool to room temperature. Wrap tightly in plastic wrap so it will keep a round shape; freeze just until it is firm enough to slice.

Slice the tenderloin paper thin on a meat slicer or a kitchen mandolin. Arrange on a platter over a bed of arugula, garnish with Zippy Mayonnaise. Sprinkle with Parmesan cheese and parsley.

Yield. Serves 4 to 6

BLT Skewers and Buttermilk Dressing

8 wooden or metal skewers
8 slices bacon, sliced thick
1/3 cup lemon juice
1/3 cup olive oil
2 tablespoons fresh basil, chopped
1/4 teaspoon salt
1/8 teaspoon pepper
1 cup cherry tomatoes
2 medium avocados, halved, seeded, peeled and cut into 1 inch pieces
8 ounces ciabatta bread, cut into 1 inch cubes
romaine lettuce, cored, washed and dried
Buttermilk Ranch Dressing (see recipe in section "Salads and Dressings")

Note: If you are using wooden skewers soak them several hours in water to prevent them from burning.

Preheat the grill to medium.

Fry the bacon over medium high heat in a skillet until it is cooked about halfway. It needs to be pliable enough to bend on the skewers.

In a large bowl whisk together the lemon juice, olive oil, basil, salt and pepper. Add the tomatoes and avocado pieces to the mixture, tossing gently to coat. Transfer to another bowl using a slotted spoon and set aside. Toss the bread cubes with the remaining mixture; remove and set aside. Reserve any lemon mixture.

Alternately thread the bacon, tomatoes, avocado pieces and bread cubes onto the skewers accordion style.

Grill until the bread is golden and the bacon is crisp turning only once.

Brush the lettuce leaves with any remaining lemon mixture. Serve the skewers over the lettuce leaves taco style and drizzle with Buttermilk Ranch Dressing.

Yield: Serves 8

As a little girl I remember that Deviled Eggs were part of every social gathering or holiday meal. My Mother put sweet pickles in hers along with a dash of juice from the pickle jar as well. This is a totally different recipe but it has become a big hit at our family events!

Cajun Deviled Eggs

12 large eggs, boiled
1/2 cup mayonnaise
1 1/2 tablespoons Creole mustard
2 tablespoons celery, finely minced
salt and pepper to taste
1 tablespoon fresh dill, finely chopped
Cajun Seasoning (see recipe in section "Sauces and Seasonings")

Peel the boiled eggs and cut in half lengthwise.

Scoop out the yolks, saving the whites and set them aside. Transfer the yolks to a bowl and mash with a fork. Add the mayonnaise, Creole mustard, celery, salt and pepper; mix well. Neatly spoon the yolk mixture back into the whites.

Garnish with the fresh dill and lightly sprinkle the Cajun Seasoning over the eggs.

Yield: Serves 12

This recipe is a great use for all of the wonderful ripe tomatoes that we have an abundance of in the summer time. If I'm not roasting the tomatoes to freeze for later use then I'm making salsa or bruschetta! It is one of our favorite appetizers to take along on our five o'clock cocktail cruises around the lake!

Garlic and Tomato Salsa

2 1/2 pounds tomatoes, diced and drained (about 8 medium tomatoes)
2 heaping tablespoons garlic, minced
2 teaspoons kosher salt
1/2 medium red onion, finely diced
1 small jalapeño pepper, seeded and minced
juice of 1 lime
1/4 cup fresh cilantro, minced
1 tablespoon honey
black pepper
Tabasco sauce to taste
tortilla chips

Dice the tomatoes and place them in a fine sieve over a medium size bowl in order for the tomatoes to drain of their extra juices. Discard the juice or save for another use. In the medium bowl add the drained tomatoes, garlic, salt, red onion, jalapeño pepper, lime juice, cilantro, honey, black pepper and Tabasco sauce; mix well. Refrigerate and marinade for a couple of hours before serving. You may need to drain any extra juice that has accumulated at the bottom of the bowl again. Serve with tortilla chips.

Yield: Serves 6

Shredded Pork on Roasted Pepper Wedges

1 pound pork tenderloin
juice of 1 lime
2 tablespoons garlic, minced
2 tablespoons Mexican Seasoning (see recipe in section "Sauces and Seasonings")
3 tablespoons vegetable oil
2 red bell peppers
2 yellow bell peppers
1 jar (16 ounces) taco sauce
2 tablespoons chipotle peppers in Adobo sauce, finely chopped
16 ounces sharp cheddar cheese, shredded
Garnishes:
1/2 cup cilantro, chopped
1/2 cup green onions, chopped
1/4 cup black olives, pitted and chopped

Place the pork in a baking dish and squeeze the lime over it. Spread the garlic over the pork evenly. Marinade for at least 4 hours while refrigerating.

Preheat oven to 350 degrees.

Bring the pork to room temperature and drain off excess juice and discard. Coat the Mexican Seasoning generously over the pork and massage in well. Heat the oil in a medium skillet over medium high heat until hot. Add the pork and brown on all sides. Turn meat as it releases itself from the pan. Do not force. Once it has nicely browned return to a clean baking dish and place in preheated oven for 25 to 30 minutes or until internal temperature is 145 degrees. Remove pork from oven and set aside to rest for at least 20 minutes.

Using two forks, shred the pork. If shredded pieces are too long lightly chop until pork is about 1 inch in length.

Cut the tops off of the peppers, clean out the seeds and white membrane. Cut the peppers into 1/8's lengthwise and then cut into 1/2's. You should have the perfect bite size pieces at this point.

In a medium size bowl mix the taco sauce and chipotle peppers in Adobo sauce together; set aside.

Place pepper wedges on 2 large foil lined baking sheets with skin side down. Place a generous spoonful of pork on each pepper wedge and top with a heaping tablespoon of sauce.

Bake in the oven for 35 minutes or until peppers are tender and pork is heated through. Remove from oven and top with shredded cheese. Place back in the oven and bake just until cheese is melted while watching carefully. Transfer to a serving platter. Top off each pepper wedge with a spoonful of sauce. Garnish with cilantro, green onions and olives.

Yield: Serves 8

Baby Quiches

3 ounces cream cheese, softened
1/2 cup butter, softened
1 cup flour
1/4 cup Swiss cheese, grated
6 green onions, chopped
1/2 pound bacon, cooked and crumbled
1 cup heavy cream
2 eggs, beaten

Preheat oven to 325 degrees. Prepare miniature muffin pans with cooking spray and set aside.

Crust: In a medium size bowl cut the cream cheese and butter into the flour with a pastry cutter; combine well. Place in the refrigerator to chill until ready to use. When ready to bake, make tiny balls of dough and press into the prepared miniature muffin pans.

Mixture: Combine the Swiss cheese, green onions and crumbled bacon. Put a small amount of the mixture into each crust.

Filling: Whisk together the heavy cream and eggs in a small saucepan and heat over medium to medium high heat. Bring to a low simmer and remove from heat. Pour 1 teaspoon of the filling over each quiche.

Bake for 12 to 15 minutes or until lightly golden brown.

Makes 24 individual quiches.

Yield: Serves 8 to 10

Bruschetta and Crostini

3 pounds ripe tomatoes (about 9 medium sized)
2 tablespoons garlic, minced
1/2 cup onion, chopped
3 tablespoons olive oil
2 tablespoons balsamic vinegar
2 tablespoons fresh parsley, chopped
2 tablespoons fresh basil, chopped
1 teaspoon salt
1/2 teaspoon pepper
1/2 cup Parmesan cheese, shredded
1 loaf Italian bread, sliced

Dice the tomatoes and place them in a fine sieve over a medium size bowl in order for the tomatoes to drain of their extra juices. Discard the juice or save for another use. In the medium bowl add the drained tomatoes, garlic, onion, oil, balsamic vinegar, parsley, basil, salt and pepper; mix well. Refrigerate and marinade for a couple of hours before serving. You may need to drain any extra juice that has accumulated at the bottom of the bowl again. Just before serving sprinkle the Parmesan cheese over the bruschetta.

Make the crostini by brushing olive oil on both sides of the sliced Italian bread. Place on a baking sheet and toast under the broiler while watching it carefully so it doesn't over brown. When the first side is golden brown turn over to toast the second side. Spread bruschetta on the crostini and serve.

Yield: Serves 6

Captain Ollen's Dangerous Marinated Conch

6 conchs (shucked) meat cleaned and sliced thin
1 medium onion, finely chopped
1 green bell pepper, finely chopped
4 stalks celery, finely chopped
1 scotch bonnet pepper, finely chopped
5 ounces Jamaican Picka Pepper sauce
1/2 cup Worcestershire sauce
1/2 cup ketchup
1 teaspoon black pepper
juice of 2 limes

Add all of the ingredients together in a medium size bowl and mix well. Refrigerate for at least two hours or more. Serve with saltine crackers.

Yield: Serves 6 to 8

Guacamole Dip

1 medium tomato, seeded and diced
1/4 medium red onion, finely chopped
1 1/2 tablespoons garlic, minced
1 small jalapeño pepper, seeded and minced
2 1/2 tablespoons fresh cilantro, finely chopped
3 avocados, ripe
1 1/2 teaspoons kosher salt
black pepper, freshly ground
juice of 1 lime
Tabasco sauce
tortilla chips

Combine the tomato, onion, garlic, jalapeño and cilantro together in a medium size bowl and mix together. Cut the avocados in half lengthwise avoiding the center pit. Twist the two halves apart, remove the pit and scoop out the flesh. In a separate bowl mash the avocados just until you have a chunky texture. Fold in the tomato mixture. Season with salt, pepper, lime juice and Tabasco sauce. Stir gently to combine. Serve with tortilla chips.

Yield: Serves 6

Jalapeno Cheese Squares

I have been making this recipe for as long as I can remember. It is always a big hit with the crowd even for those of you who are not hot heads!

1 jar (12 ounces) sliced jalapeño peppers, drained
2 pounds sharp cheddar cheese, grated
12 eggs, beaten

Preheat oven to 350 degrees.

Prepare a 13x9x2 inch baking dish with cooking spray.

Place a layer of the sliced jalapeños on the bottom of the baking dish. Sprinkle the cheese over the peppers and pour the eggs evenly over the top. Bake for one hour or until golden brown.

Cool slightly and cut into two inch squares.

Serve warm or at room temperature. Makes about 24 squares.

Yield: Serves 12

Pimiento and Cheese Dip

16 ounces extra sharp cheddar cheese, shredded
8 ounces cream cheese, softened
1 cup heavy whipping cream
1 jar (8 ounces) pimientos, drained
1/4 cup green onions, thinly sliced
1/8 teaspoon ground cayenne pepper
1/4 teaspoon garlic powder
4 tablespoons butter
1 loaf French baguette bread, sliced

In a medium size saucepan over low heat add first three ingredients and heat until melted and blended together to form a smooth sauce. Add the pimientos, green onions, cayenne pepper and garlic powder. Stir to combine. Keep warm over very low heat. Serve hot with buttered and toasted French baguette bread. Makes 2 cups.

Yield: Serves 8

Roasted Garlic

What's a little misunderstanding between good friends?

2 large bulbs garlic
olive oil
salt and pepper

Preheat oven to 375 degrees.

Cut off the top of each bulb of garlic, slicing into the points of the cloves. Place the garlic cut side up on a piece of foil. Drizzle with olive oil and sprinkle with salt and pepper. Wrap the foil up around the bulbs and bake for 45 to 60 minutes, or until they release their perfume. Open the foil and test for doneness. The cloves should squeeze softly when pinched. Serve by spreading on a slice of toasted Italian bread.

This can be used in most dishes that call for garlic. It may be just a bit stronger since it has been roasted, therefore using less may be necessary.

Roasted garlic will keep for several days in the refrigerator.

Yield: Serves 8 to 10

Salmon Squares

Crust:
1 1/2 cups whole wheat flour
1/2 teaspoon salt
1/2 teaspoon paprika
3/4 cup cold butter, cut into small cubes
1 cup cheddar cheese, shredded
1/4 cup walnuts, chopped

Filling:
16 ounces fresh salmon
salt and pepper to taste
3 eggs
1 cup sour cream
1/4 cup mayonnaise
2 tablespoons shallots, finely chopped
2 teaspoons fresh dill, chopped
1 teaspoon Tabasco sauce
1/2 cup cheddar cheese, shredded
fresh dill, chopped for garnish

Preheat oven to 400 degrees.

In a medium size bowl combine the whole wheat flour, salt and paprika. Cut in the butter with a pastry cutter or fork until crumbly. Stir in 1 cup of cheese and the walnuts. Set aside 1 cup of the crumb mixture for the topping. Press remaining crumb mixture into the bottom and up the sides of a square 10x10 inch baking pan.

Place the salmon on a piece of aluminum foil cut large enough to completely wrap the fish while baking. Add salt and pepper, wrap in foil and place on a baking sheet. Bake in oven for 12 minutes. Remove from oven and let salmon rest for another 10 minutes while still wrapped in foil. Let cool to room temperature and gently flake apart with a fork.

In a medium size bowl beat the eggs with an electric mixer until whipped. Add sour cream, mayonnaise, shallots, dill and Tabasco sauce; stir to combine well. Fold in 1/2 cup of cheese and the flaked salmon.

Spoon into the pan over the crumb crust. Sprinkle the top with the remaining one cup of crumb mixture. Bake for 30 minutes until puffy. Let stand 10 minutes before serving. Cut into squares and serve warm. Garnish with fresh chopped dill.

Yield: Serves 12 as appetizer or 8 as entree

Shrimp Ceviche-Style

This is an excellent dish that can be served as either an appetizer, salad or entree! Its best when it's prepared the day before serving. The flavors are enhanced two-fold the second day!

1 pound small frozen shrimp (150/250 count), cooked, peeled and deveined
1/2 cup tomato, diced
1/4 cup red onion, diced
2 stalks green onion, diced
1 tablespoon parsley, chopped
2 tablespoons cilantro, chopped
1/2 cup cucumber, chopped
1 medium avocado, cut into bite size pieces
1 tablespoon garlic, minced
juice of 1 lime
1/8 teaspoon crushed red pepper or to taste
salt and pepper to taste
Tabasco sauce to taste
1 loaf of French baguette bread, sliced
olive oil

Defrost the shrimp in a colander with cold water running over it. Once it is completely thawed and completely drained of excess water place it in a medium size bowl. Add the tomato, onion, green onion, parsley, cilantro, cucumber, avocado and garlic. Squeeze the lime juice over all of the ingredients and season to taste with crushed red pepper, salt and pepper. Sprinkle with the Tabasco sauce to taste. Toss gently to combine. Cover and refrigerate. Marinade for at least 6 hours or more, preferably overnight.

Stir gently once again before serving and add more lime juice if needed. Serve cold over toasted French baguette slices.

Note: You can also serve this on crackers, lettuce cups or hallowed out tomatoes.

Yield: Serves 12 as appetizer or 6 as entree

Hot Crabmeat Canapés

1/2 pound lump crabmeat
6 tablespoons mayonnaise
1/2 teaspoon salt
1 tablespoon onion, minced
juice of 1 lemon
1 tablespoon Worcestershire sauce
1/2 cup Parmesan cheese, finely grated
3 dozen bread squares, toasted
paprika

Place the first 7 ingredients in a medium size bowl and stir to combine. Spread the mixture on the toasted bread squares and sprinkle with the paprika. Place on a cooking sheet under the broiler until bubbly and lightly golden brown. Serve immediately.

Yield: Serves 12 to 18

Spinach, Artichoke and Water Chestnut Dip

1 package (10 ounces) frozen chopped spinach
1 jar (6 1/2 ounces) marinated artichokes, drained and chopped
1 can (8 1/2 ounces) water chestnuts, drained and chopped
1 cup mayonnaise
1 cup sour cream
1 envelope vegetable soup mix
1/2 small onion, minced
2 dashes Tabasco sauce

Thaw the spinach completely and squeeze all of the water out with your hands. The spinach needs to be very dry. In a medium size bowl add the spinach along with all of the other ingredients and blend well. Refrigerate overnight. Serve on crackers.

Yield: Serves 8 to 10

Salads and Dressings

Corn and Black Bean Salad

12 ears corn on the cob, steamed, cooled and kernels removed from the cob (about 6 cups kernels)
1 medium yellow sweet pepper, diced
1 medium red sweet pepper, diced
1 cucumber, peeled and diced
1/2 pint cherry tomatoes, halved
1 can (15 ounces) black beans, rinsed and drained
1/2 bunch green onions, chopped
1/2 medium red onion, chopped
1 medium jalapeño pepper, seeded and finely chopped
dash of Tabasco sauce
3 tablespoons cilantro, finely chopped
2 tablespoons parsley, finely chopped
2 teaspoons oregano, finely chopped
2 tablespoons garlic, finely chopped
juice of 2 limes
1/4 cup olive oil
salt and pepper
pinch crushed red pepper

In a medium size bowl combine the corn, sweet peppers, cucumber, tomatoes, black beans, green onions, red onions and jalapeño pepper. Stir to combine.

In a small bowl whisk together the Tabasco sauce, cilantro, parsley, oregano, garlic, lime juice, olive oil, salt, pepper and crushed red pepper. Pour over the vegetables and gently stir.

Cover and marinade for one hour in the refrigerator. Serve cold.

Yield: Serves 10 to 12

Roasted Beet and Chèvre Stacks with Oranges

12 ounces Chèvre (goat cheese), softened
2 tablespoons fresh thyme, minced
6 medium beets (about 1 pound), roasted
3 large naval oranges (2 for segments and 1 for zest and juice)
2 tablespoons balsamic vinegar glaze
6 large basil leaves
2 ounces walnuts, chopped

In a small bowl combine the softened cheese and the minced thyme, mix well. Place the cheese on a piece of plastic wrap and form into a tidy tube shape about 1 1/2 inches thick. Wrap and refrigerate for at least 2 hours or until firm.

Assemble the roasted beet stacks by slicing the beets into 1/4 inch rounds. Set aside the rounded ends of the beets so your stacks will sit flat. Slice the cold and firm cheese into about 16 slices that are 1/8 inch thick. Make 6 stacks by alternating the layers of beets and cheese on top of each other starting with a slice of beet on the bottom and ending with a slice of beet on top. Arrange the stacks on a platter.

Peel and slice 2 of the naval oranges while completely removing the white bitter pith. Separate each segment and cut into bite size pieces. Arrange the orange pieces around the beet stacks. Cut the rounded ends of the beets that you set aside into bite size pieces and add them to the platter with the oranges.

Zest the remaining orange (again avoiding the white bitter pith) and set aside. Squeeze the orange juice over the top of the beet stacks. Drizzle the balsamic vinegar glaze over the top and sprinkle with the orange zest. Stack the basil leaves on top of each other and roll cigar style and slice crosswise, creating ribbons. Sprinkle the basil ribbons and the chopped walnuts over the top of the beets.

Serve immediately as the beets will stain the cheese if it sits for a long period of time.

Note: If you aren't able to buy the beets pre-roasted you can roast your own by washing them thoroughly and wrapping in aluminum foil. Place in a preheated oven at 350 degrees for about 1 hour or until tender. Let cool, unwrap and gently remove the skin while wearing plastic gloves or using paper towels. Use caution as the beets will stain clothing and your fingers very easily.

Yield: Serves 6

Antipasta Salad

1 large head of broccoli
2 pints cherry tomatoes
32 ounces mozzarella cheese, cut into bite size cubes
1 pound salami, sliced thick and cut into bite size cubes
1 pound pepperoni, sliced thick and cut into bite size cubes
24 ounces marinated artichoke hearts, drained
12 ounces red pimientos, drained and sliced
12 ounces pepperoncini or banana peppers, drained
12 ounces marinated Kalamata olives, pitted and drained
3 1/2 ounces capers, drained
1 large red onion, cut into wedges
1 1/2 tablespoons Italian seasoning
1/3 cup Italian dressing

Wash the broccoli and trim the florets from the stalks. Cut florets into bite size pieces (not to small). Place the broccoli in a very large bowl. Wash the cherry tomatoes and add them to the bowl. Add all of the additional ingredients and mix well. Cover and refrigerate to marinade for at least 2 hours. Stir once more before serving and check seasonings. Add more Italian dressing if desired.

Yield: Serves 24

Arugula and Pear Salad

This is a yummy salad and a family favorite. You would never guess from the ingredients of the dressing that it's as tasty as it is. You have to try it to believe it!

1/4 cup of red wine vinegar
1/4 cup of Equal (artificial sweetener)
1 large bag (10 ounces) arugula, washed and dried
2 ripe pears, peeled and sliced
1 cup Maytag blue cheese, crumbled
1 cup glazed sweet walnuts

In a small jar add the red wine vinegar and Equal; shake until completely dissolved and mixed well.

In a large salad bowl add the arugula, pears, Maytag blue cheese and walnuts. Just before serving shake the dressing once again to insure it is combined. Pour just enough dressing over the salad to lightly coat and gently toss together. Serve immediately.

Yield: Serves 8

Arugula, Watermelon and Feta Cheese Salad

Vinaigrette:
1/4 cup lemon juice
1/4 cup orange juice
1/4 cup shallots, minced
1 tablespoon honey
1 teaspoon kosher salt
1/2 teaspoon freshly ground black pepper
1/2 cup olive oil

Salad:
4 cups seedless watermelon, largely diced
2 cups grape tomatoes
1 cup feta cheese, coarsely crumbled
1/2 cup red onion, chopped
1/2 cup fresh basil, thinly sliced
1/2 cup fresh mint, thinly sliced
1 package (5 ounces) arugula
1 package (5 ounces) baby spinach

To prepare the dressing combine all of the ingredients together in a medium size bowl with the exception of the olive oil. While continuously whisking slowly add the olive oil. Whisk until completely blended together.

Assemble the salad by combining all of the ingredients in a large salad bowl. Dress lightly with the vinaigrette and toss gently to combine. Serve immediately in chilled salad bowls.

Yield: Serves 12

Buttermilk Ranch Dressing

1 1/4 cups mayonnaise
3/4 cup buttermilk
2 teaspoons red wine vinegar
1 1/2 teaspoons garlic, minced
3 tablespoons fresh chives, finely chopped
2 teaspoons lemon pepper
1/2 cup Parmesan cheese
1 teaspoon salt
freshly ground black pepper to taste
1 teaspoon Cajun seasoning (see recipe in section "Sauces and Seasonings")

Whisk all of the ingredients together in a bowl. Cover with plastic wrap and refrigerate until ready to use.

Yield: Makes 2 cups

Caesar Salad

This is the best room at the cottage!

1 clove garlic, peeled
2 egg yolks
2 tablespoons lemon juice
6 tablespoons olive oil
1/2 tablespoon anchovy paste
1 tablespoon Worcestershire sauce
salt and freshly ground pepper
1 large head of romaine lettuce, washed, dried and torn into bite size pieces
1 cup Parmesan cheese, shredded
Roasted Garlic Croutons (see recipe in this section)

Rub the inside of wooden salad bowl with the garlic and discard. In the same salad bowl continuously whisk the egg yolk together while gradually adding the lemon juice and the olive oil. Stir in the anchovy paste and the Worcestershire sauce. Salt and pepper to taste. Add the lettuce to the bowl and toss together. Garnish with the cheese and Roasted Garlic Croutons. Serve immediately.

Yield: Serves 4

Green Pea and Wagon Wheel Pasta Salad

1 pound wagon wheel pasta, mini
3 packages (10 ounces each) frozen green peas
1 package (8 ounces) mushrooms, sliced
1 package (5 ounces) fresh baby spinach
1 medium yellow onion, chopped
2 cups sharp cheddar cheese, shredded
2 1/2 cups mayonnaise
salt and pepper to taste

Cook the pasta in salted boiling water according to the package directions. Drain the pasta in a colander and rinse under cold water to stop the cooking process. Drain the pasta well as it needs to be completely dry before assembling the salad; set aside.

Add the frozen green peas to a colander and rinse under cold water to thaw. Thaw and drain completely; set aside.

Once the pasta and the peas are dry place them in a very large bowl along with the remaining ingredients. Gently combine; add salt and pepper to taste. Refrigerate for at least 2 hours.

Just before serving, stir the salad and check once more for seasoning. Add more mayonnaise if needed.

Serve cold.

Note: Chopped boiled eggs are also a nice addition to this salad.

Yield: Serves 12 to 16

Layered Spinach Salad

2 cups mayonnaise
1 cup sour cream
1 teaspoon lemon juice
1 cup Swiss cheese, shredded
1 bag (10 ounces) fresh baby spinach, washed, dried and chilled
1/2 pound bacon, cut into 1 inch pieces and cooked
1 package (10 ounces) frozen green peas
1/2 head of iceberg lettuce, washed, dried, torn into pieces and chilled
3 hard boiled eggs, peeled and chopped
1/2 medium onion, chopped
1/4 teaspoon sugar
salt and pepper to taste

Combine the mayonnaise, sour cream, lemon juice and Swiss cheese in a medium size bowl; mix well and set aside. Make layers in a large casserole dish or glass bowl beginning with the spinach. Add the bacon, uncooked frozen green peas, iceberg lettuce, eggs and onion. Sprinkle the salad with sugar, salt and pepper. Top with the dressing (if the bowl is narrow at the top all of the dressing may not be needed). Cover the salad with plastic wrap and refrigerate overnight. Toss before serving.

Yield: Serves 12

Macaroni Salad

According to my Mother-in-law Ruthie, the trick to this recipe is for all of the ingredients to be dry so the mayonnaise sticks to the pasta, celery and onions.

1 pound elbow macaroni
1 1/2 cups celery, chopped
1 1/2 cups onions, chopped
4 eggs, hard boiled and peeled
2 1/2 cups mayonnaise
salt and pepper to taste

Cook the macaroni according to the package directions for al dente. Immediately remove from heat and drain the pasta in a colander and rinse under cold water to stop the cooking process. Leave the macaroni in the colander sitting on a clean dish towel and refrigerate uncovered along with the celery, onions and eggs. Refrigerate overnight so they become cold and dry. Chop the eggs on the morning of the day you are serving the salad. Place all of the ingredients in a large bowl and combine well. Refrigerate again until ready to serve. Stir once again just before serving and adjust the salt and pepper if needed. You may need to add more mayonnaise at this point if the pasta seems a little dry. Serve cold.

Yield: Serves 12

Maytag Blue Cheese Dressing

2 cups mayonnaise
3 tablespoons apple cider vinegar
1 teaspoon Worcestershire sauce
2 tablespoons lemon juice
1 teaspoon dry mustard
freshly ground pepper to taste
1/4 teaspoon celery seed
1 cup crumbled Maytag blue cheese

Whisk together all of the ingredients but the blue cheese in a bowl. Gently stir in the blue cheese without disturbing the chunky texture. Cover and refrigerate until ready to use.

Yield: Makes 2 cups

Roasted Garlic Croutons

1 loaf day old bread, cut into bite size cubes
3/4 cup olive oil
5 cloves garlic, peeled and minced
1/4 teaspoon marjoram
1/4 teaspoon thyme
pinch salt

Preheat oven to 350 degrees.

In a large bowl toss the bread cubes with the olive oil, garlic, marjoram, thyme and salt.

Spread the bread cubes evenly on a baking sheet without crowding. Cook in two batches if necessary and bake for 15 minutes. Toss again and bake for an additional 15 minutes.

Use as a garnish for salads and soups.

Note: Be adventurous with your spices. You can use just about any spice to change it up occasionally according to what you are cooking and the season.

Yield: Serves 8

Ruthie's Fruit Salad

It wouldn't be a proper holiday meal at our house without Ruthie's Fruit Salad! It is steadfast comfort food for my husband as his Mom always had this dish at each and every holiday table. Here's to our dear sweet Ruthie!

1 can (16 ounces) pineapple chunks, drained
1 package (10 ounces) miniature marshmallows
1 can (16 ounces) fruit cocktail
2 cups grapes, seedless
24 ounces whipped topping

The night before serving combine the drained pineapple chunks and the marshmallows in a medium size bowl, cover and leave to marinade overnight in the refrigerator.

The day of serving combine the fruit cocktail, grapes and whipped topping to the pineapple and marshmallow mixture. Gently fold together. Keep covered and refrigerate until ready to serve.

Yield: Serves 10 to 12

Tuna, White Bean and Quinoa Salad

1 1/2 cups quinoa, cooked
1/3 cup olive oil
juice of 2 lemons
2 teaspoons garlic, minced
2 teaspoons Dijon mustard
1 teaspoon crushed red pepper
1 can (15 ounces) cannellini beans, rinsed
1 can (12 ounces) tuna, all white, packed in water and drained
1/4 cup red onion, chopped
3/4 cup celery, chopped
1/2 cup parsley, chopped
1/4 cup tarragon, chopped
salt and pepper
6 romaine lettuce leaves or 6 large ripe tomatoes

Cook quinoa according to package directions and set aside to cool.

In a large bowl whisk together the olive oil, lemon juice, garlic, Dijon mustard and crushed red pepper. Add the cooked quinoa, beans, tuna, onion, celery, parsley and tarragon. Season with salt and pepper to taste. Toss to combine well. Cover and refrigerate or serve immediately.

Serve in romaine lettuce leaves taco style or hollowed out tomatoes on a bed of lettuce.

Yield: Serves 6

Champagne and Shallot Vinaigrette Dressing

2 tablespoons shallots, finely chopped
1/2 teaspoon coarse salt
2 tablespoons champagne vinegar
6 tablespoons canola oil
1 tablespoon fresh herbs, minced (your choice of parsley, chives, tarragon or basil)

Add the shallots, salt and vinegar to a small bowl; stir to combine. Once the salt is dissolved slowly add the oil while whisking to combine. Add the minced herbs of choice and whisk again before serving. Pour a small amount over clean dry salad greens and toss to combine.

Yield: Makes 1/2 cup

Southern Slaw

1 head of cabbage, shredded
3 large carrots, grated
1/2 cup sugar
1 tablespoon prepared mustard
1/4 cup white vinegar
1 teaspoon salt
3/4 cup vegetable oil

Place the shredded cabbage and grated carrots in a large bowl and set aside. In a small mixing bowl add the sugar, mustard, vinegar, salt and oil; whisk together. Pour over the cabbage and carrots, gently toss to combine.

Cover with plastic wrap and refrigerate. Marinade for several hours or overnight before serving.

Serve cold.

Yield: Serves 8 to 10

Tomato and Cucumber Salad

2 large tomatoes, chopped
1 small onion, chopped
2 cucumbers, peeled and chopped
1/2 cup fresh parsley, chopped
1 tablespoon olive oil
juice of 1 lemon
salt and pepper to taste

Place the chopped tomatoes in a fine sieve over a small bowl in order for them to drain of their extra juices. Discard the juice. In a medium bowl add the tomatoes and the remaining vegetables. Add the oil, lemon juice and season with salt and pepper. Refrigerate until ready to serve.

Yield: Serves 4

Vinaigrette Dressing

1/2 cup olive oil
3 tablespoons wine vinegar, balsamic vinegar or lemon juice
salt and pepper
1 large shallot, minced
2 tablespoons fresh herbs, minced (your choice of parsley, chives, tarragon or basil)
optional: 1 teaspoon mustard

Combine all of the ingredients in a small jar with a lid and shake to combine well. Pour a small amount over clean dry salad greens and gently toss.

Yield: Makes 3/4 cup

Breakfast and Sandwiches

Lemon Drop Dutch Pancake

Pancake:
4 tablespoons butter
4 large eggs
1/2 cup all purpose flour
1/2 cup half and half

Topping:
2 tablespoons butter, melted
juice of 1 lemon
4 tablespoons powdered sugar

Preheat oven to 425 degrees.

Melt the butter in a 9 or 10 inch cast iron skillet and swirl around to coat the sides evenly; set aside. You can also use any oven proof non-stick skillet of the same size or a pie plate.

In a blender mix together the eggs, flour, and half and half until well combined.

Pour the egg mixture into the skillet. Place the skillet in the oven and bake for 20 to 25 minutes. The mixture will rise and puff around the edges. The pancake is ready when the center looks set and the edges have risen and turned golden brown.

Remove from the oven. Immediately drizzle the melted butter and lemon juice over the pancake. Sprinkle generously with the powdered sugar.

Serve hot.

Yield: Serves 2

Sautéed Mushrooms, Spinach and Baked Eggs

2 tablespoons butter
1 tablespoon shallots, minced
1 teaspoon garlic, minced
2 cups mushrooms, sliced
1 package (5 ounces) fresh spinach
1/4 cup heavy cream
salt and pepper
2 eggs
1/4 teaspoon thyme
fresh parsley, chopped for garnish

Preheat oven to 400 degrees.

In a medium size oven proof skillet melt the butter over medium high heat. When the foam has subsided add the shallots and cook until tender and translucent. Add the garlic and cook for 1 minute. Add the mushrooms and cook until golden brown. Add the spinach and cook until wilted. Salt and pepper to taste.

Reduce the heat to medium and add the heavy cream. Heat just until the cream is hot. Make 2 shallow wells in the mushroom mixture and crack 1 egg into each well. Sprinkle with the thyme. Transfer to the oven and cook until egg whites have just set, about 5 to 7 minutes.

Serve over crispy hash browns or oven toasted buttered bread. Garnish with fresh parsley.

Note: If the eggs are cooked sunny side up they add to the sauce of the dish when the yolks are broken.

Yield: Serves 2

Banana Compote

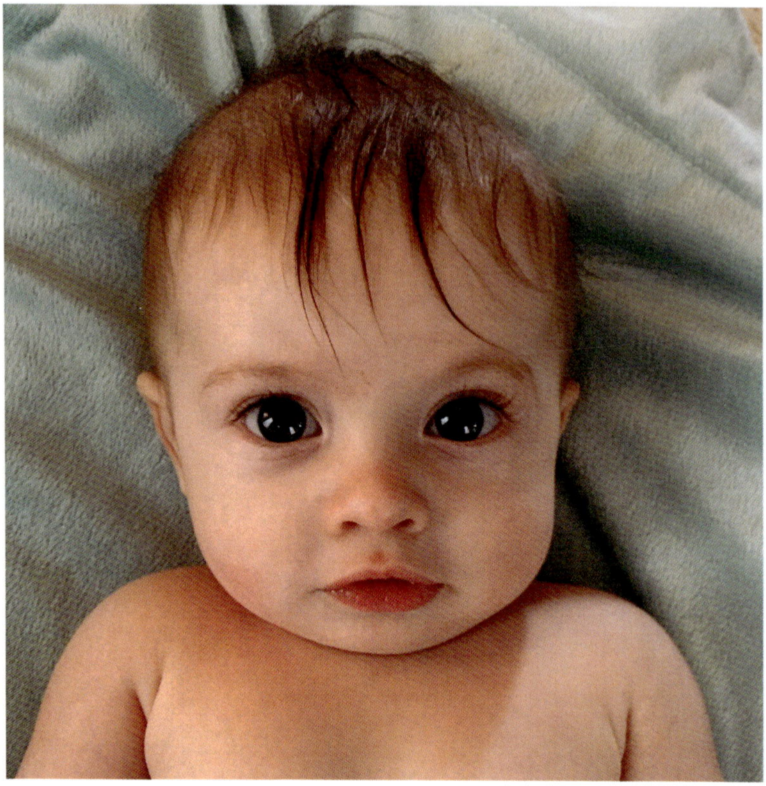

Meet the newest addition to our family!

4 tablespoons butter
3 tablespoons brown sugar
1 banana, sliced on the bias
2 tablespoons maple syrup
1 tablespoon walnuts, chopped (optional)

Melt the butter in a medium size skillet over medium heat. When the foam subsides add the brown sugar and stir to dissolve. Add the sliced banana, maple syrup and walnuts; stir well to combine. Heat through and serve immediately over french toast, pancakes or even ice cream!

Yield: Serves 2

Chicken Salad

This recipe is a little bit off the beaten path from your normal every day chicken salad. I love the taste that the Dijon mustard gives this dish. It has just that little bit of a twist and a zip that other similar recipes don't have. I also like using the leftover chicken from the recipe "Lemon and Rosemary Roasted Chicken" (see recipe in section "Main Dishes").

3 1/2 cups chicken breast, cooked and diced
3/4 cup celery, finely chopped
1/2 cup onions, finely chopped
2 tablespoons fresh parsley, minced
1/4 teaspoon celery seed
2 tablespoons Dijon mustard
1/2 cup mayonnaise
salt and pepper to taste

Add all of the ingredients to a medium size bowl and combine well. Serve with sliced tomatoes as a salad or on toasted bread.

Yield: Serves 6

Creamed Chipped Beef and Eggs

6 eggs, hard boiled and peeled
4 tablespoons butter
4 tablespoons flour
salt and pepper to taste
2 cups whole milk
1 1/4 cups dried beef, chopped
4 slices country white bread, toasted
pinch paprika
1 tablespoon fresh parsley, minced

Chop the eggs and set aside. Melt the butter in a large skillet over medium heat. Once the foam subsides slowly stir in the flour until it becomes a thick paste. Add salt and pepper, cook for a few minutes while stirring constantly. Gradually add the milk and continue stirring to keep the sauce smooth. Cook over medium low heat until the sauce thickens. Add the eggs and the dried beef. Heat through and taste for seasonings. Serve over toast and garnish with paprika and parsley.

Note: Once the eggs are added only cook long enough to heat through. The eggs will become tough if cooked too long. Monitor your salt carefully when making the sauce because the beef is preserved so it is naturally on the salty side.

Yield: Serves 4

French Baked Eggs

For each serving:
2 teaspoons butter, divided
2 tablespoons heavy cream
2 eggs
salt and pepper
1/2 teaspoon fresh parsley, minced

Preheat oven to 375 degrees. Butter a 4 inch ramekin. Add 1 tablespoon of cream to the ramekin and set in 1/2 inch of simmering water in an oven proof pan over medium high heat. When the cream is hot break the eggs into the ramekin. Pour the remaining spoonful of cream over the eggs and top with the remaining butter.

Place on the middle rack of the oven and bake for 10 to 12 minutes. The eggs are done when they are just set but still tremble slightly in the ramekin. They will set a little more when the ramekin is removed so they should not be overcooked.

Season with salt and pepper. Garnish with the parsley.

Note: The ramekin may remain in the pan of hot water out of the oven for 10 to 15 minutes before serving. To prevent overcooking remove the eggs from the oven when slightly underdone.

Yield: Serves 1

Ham with Red Eye Gravy

3 tablespoons butter
8 slices ham, thickly cut
1 cup black coffee, lightly sweetened

Melt the butter in a large skillet over medium heat. Fry the ham slices for 2 minutes on each side or until lightly browned. Set aside and keep warm. Increase the heat under the skillet to medium high and add the coffee. Scrape up the browned bits left from the ham; reduce the heat to low. Simmer gently for 2 minutes or until it has thickened and is a bit syrupy. Serve over grits, biscuits or ham.

Yield: Serves 4

Miniature Egg Souffles

2 tablespoons butter
2 eggs, beaten
1 teaspoon ice water
1 tablespoon sour cream
1/2 teaspoon baking powder
1 tablespoon fresh parsley, minced and divided
1/2 teaspoon salt
2 dashes Tabasco sauce
1/2 cup cheddar cheese, grated

Preheat oven to 350 degrees.

Grease 2 individual 4 inch ramekins with the butter.

Combine all of the ingredients in a small bowl (reserving 1/2 tablespoon of parsley for garnish); mix well. Pour evenly into the prepared ramekins. Bake in the oven until puffed and firm, about 12 to 15 minutes.

Garnish with fresh minced parsley.

Yield: Serves 2

Oatmeal in a Jar

We make an assembly line with the mason jars and add the different ingredients before we go to bed. The next morning you have a refreshing breakfast ready whether you are on the run or having a leisurely breakfast at home. You can get creative with your choice of fruit and other ingredients so be adventurous!

1/3 cup uncooked quick oats (not instant and not flavored)
1/2 teaspoon chia seeds
1/2 teaspoon ground flaxseed
1/2 teaspoon wheat germ
1/4 teaspoon ground cinnamon
2/3 cup milk (any kind)
3 tablespoons yogurt, any flavor
1/3 banana, sliced
1/4 cup fresh fruit of choice, blueberries, strawberries, etc.
1 tablespoon honey

Garnish: granola, bran buds, slivered almonds or chopped nuts of your choice

Place first 5 dry ingredients in a 12 ounce jar with a tight fitting lid, cover and shake gently. Finish by adding last 5 ingredients, cover and shake once again. Refrigerate overnight. Shake again next morning and add garnish of your choice.

Make one jar for each person.

Note: No need to cook! Serve cold and enjoy!

Yield: Serves 1

Pimiento and Cheese Sandwiches

2 pounds mild cheddar cheese, shredded
2 jars (7 ounces each) pimientos
1 medium onion, finely chopped
2 large dill pickles, finely chopped
4 stalks celery, finely chopped
1/8 teaspoon salt
2 cups mayonnaise
1 loaf white country bread, sliced

Place all of the ingredients into a medium size bowl and stir to combine well. Serve on white country bread with crust removed and cut on the diagonal.

Refrigerate until ready to use if you are not making the sandwiches immediately.

Yield: Serves 12

The "Maines" Toastie

For each serving:
4 tablespoons butter, divided
2 slices fresh sourdough bread
2 slices mozzarella cheese
8 slices prosciutto, thinly sliced
6 small sun dried tomatoes, packed in oil
4 basil leaves

Spread 1 tablespoon of butter on one side of each slice of bread. Meanwhile heat 2 tablespoons of butter in a heavy skillet on medium high heat. When the butter stops foaming you will know the skillet is hot enough to start cooking the sandwich. Lay one piece of bread (buttered side down) in the hot skillet. Continue quickly by adding the mozzarella cheese to the bread, following with prosciutto, sun dried tomatoes and fresh basil leaves. Top off the sandwich with the second slice of buttered bread (buttered side up). When the bottom slice is golden brown flip it over and brown the second side. When both sides are browned turn off the heat and put a lid on the pan and let the sandwich rest for about 5 minutes to insure the contents are heated through and the cheese is melted.

Yield: Serves 1

Tuna Salad Sandwich on Raisin Toast

A southern favorite! This sandwich was served at Goldsmith's Department store in Memphis, Tn. It is a cute, dainty sandwich and so very tasty. If you are partial to sweet and salty flavors together you will enjoy this combination. I have many fond memories of lunches in their restaurant after a morning of shopping and this was always my first choice.

2 eggs
1 can (12 ounces) all white tuna, packed in water
1/2 cup celery, finely chopped
1/2 cup yellow onion, finely chopped
1/2 cup mayonnaise
salt and pepper
8 slices cinnamon raisin bread
iceberg lettuce

Place two eggs in a small saucepan with just enough water to cover them. Once the eggs begin to boil immediately turn off the heat and cover with a tight fitting lid and let sit for 12 minutes.

Immediately remove the eggs from the pan and rinse under cold water. Gently crack the shell and peel away while lifting the membrane as this will allow most of the shell to release at one time. You may need to occasionally rinse the eggs with water to release any small slivers of shell.

Dice the eggs once they are completely cool and set them aside.

Drain the tuna of water and place in a medium size bowl. With a fork break up the tuna into medium fine pieces. Add the chopped celery, onion and eggs. Add the mayonnaise, salt and pepper to taste; mix well. Serve on toasted cinnamon raisin bread with fresh lettuce.

Yield: Serves 4

Vegetable Frittata

2 tablespoons olive oil
1/2 cup mushrooms, sliced
3/4 cup cherry tomatoes, cut lengthwise
8 spears cooked asparagus, diced into bite size pieces
2 cups fresh spinach
4 slices canadian bacon, cubed
4 green onions, chopped
6 to 8 eggs, beaten
salt and pepper to taste
1/2 cup freshly grated Parmesan cheese
2 tablespoons fresh herbs, minced (your choice of parsley, chives, basil or chervil)

Preheat oven to 350 degrees.

Over medium high heat warm the oil in a 8 or 10 inch cast iron skillet or other oven proof skillet. Add the mushrooms and cook until golden brown. Add the tomatoes, asparagus, spinach, canadian bacon and green onions. Cook through until spinach is wilted and ingredients are hot. Season the eggs with salt and pepper. Pour the eggs into the skillet with the vegetables. Let cook until firm around the edges. Carefully begin to lift the edges allowing the unset eggs to run underneath. The middle of the omelet will not be set at this point. Place the skillet in the oven and bake for about 10 minutes. Within just a few minutes the Frittata will be set in the center; do not over cook. Remove from oven and sprinkle with Parmesan cheese and minced herbs.

Cut into wedges and serve while hot.

Note: There is not a right and wrong in choosing the vegetable selections for a Frittata. I like to think I can clean out the refrigerator with this recipe. Other vegetables you can use are cooked swiss chard, broccoli, cauliflower, garlic, bacon, sausage, bell peppers and onions. The list goes on, just add your imagination and favorites!

Yield: Serves 4

Sauces and Seasonings

I find myself thinking that I just can't bare to lose any of the luscious herbs left in the garden when the end of summer rounds the corner and autumn is upon us. Therefore, I get busy making different combinations of pestos to freeze and use throughout the winter. I find it convenient to freeze the pesto in ice cube trays covered with a thin layer of olive oil to prevent freezer burn. When they are completely frozen I remove them from the trays, place two cubes in a small freezer bag and store in the freezer until ready to use. Some of the different combinations I like are rosemary, parsley and mint to use with lamb. Thyme, basil, parsley and oregano to use with pasta or potatoes. I also like dill and parsley to use with chicken or fish. I leave out the pine nuts, Parmesan cheese and butter if I'm freezing the pesto since you can add those items just before serving. The bonus is that by omitting those particular ingredients I can use the pesto cubes as an enhancement to other dishes. It's so convenient to grab a couple of the frozen cubes and drop them in homemade soups, stews or sauces and like magic you have that fresh herb taste in the middle of January!

Basil and Garlic Pesto

2 cups fresh basil leaves, tightly packed
1/2 cup olive oil
3 tablespoons pine nuts, toasted
2 cloves garlic, finely chopped
1/8 teaspoon salt
1/2 cup Parmesan cheese, grated
4 tablespoons butter, softened

Wash the basil thoroughly and gently pat dry with paper towels.

Add the basil, olive oil, pine nuts, garlic and salt into the bowl of a food processor and blend until you have a creamy consistency.

Transfer to a large serving bowl; mix in the cheese and softened butter by hand.

You can use the pesto on pasta, potatoes, vegetables, breads or sandwiches.

To use the pesto with pasta: toss 1 pound of hot pasta with the pesto and add up to 1/4 cup reserved cooking water (small amounts at a time) until you have the desired consistency.

Garnish with more Parmesan cheese.

Toss well to combine.

Yield: Serves 6

Brown Mustard Sauce

4 tablespoons butter, softened and divided
1/4 cup onions, finely minced
1 cup dry white wine
2 cups beef stock
3 tablespoons Dijon mustard
1/8 teaspoon sugar
3 tablespoons fresh parsley, minced

In a medium skillet over medium high heat add 1 tablespoon of the butter and heat until hot. When the foam subsides add the onions and cook until they are lightly brown and translucent.

Add the wine and boil down rapidly until it has reduced to about 1/4 cup. It should be slightly syrupy.

Add the beef stock and simmer for 10 minutes or until it is reduced by half.

Meanwhile combine the mustard, remaining 3 tablespoons of softened butter and sugar in a small bowl and cream together.

Once the beef stock has reduced remove the skillet from the heat and whisk the mustard mixture into the sauce. Stir in the parsley and serve while hot.

Serve this scrumptious sauce over hamburgers or steaks!

Yield: Serves 6

Gremolata

2 teaspoons garlic, minced
zest of 2 lemons
3 tablespoons parsley, minced
2 tablespoons bread crumbs
3 tablespoons Parmesan cheese, grated
2 tablespoons pine nuts, toasted

Make at least an hour before serving so the flavors can marry.

In a small bowl combine all of the ingredients together and mix well.

This is excellent served over vegetables like green beans, asparagus or potatoes. This should be enough sauce for 1 pound of vegetables. Also very good over chicken, red meat or fish.

You can also change it up by adding fresh mint to serve with lamb or fresh rosemary with chicken. Another tasty version would be with fresh basil to serve over sliced summer tomatoes.

Note: To toast the pine nuts add them to a sauté pan over medium low heat for 5 to 10 minutes. Toss the nuts often and remove from heat when they reach a light golden brown and you can smell the nutty aroma.

Yield: Serves 4

You should definitely wear gloves while preparing this dish! The peppers will burn your hands and absolutely don't touch your eyes until after you have washed them thoroughly!

Pat's Jerk Marinade

1 1/2 tablespoons pimiento seeds (Jamaican allspice)
2 scotch bonnet peppers, 1 pepper seeded
1 medium onion, quartered
1 medium bunch scallions, cut into medium pieces
2 inches fresh ginger, peeled and cut into 1/2 inch pieces
4 large sprigs fresh thyme
1 bulb fresh garlic, skin removed
1 teaspoon cinnamon
1/4 teaspoon ground nutmeg
1 tablespoon brown sugar
1 1/2 teaspoons black pepper
1/4 cup soy sauce
1/4 cup vegetable oil
juice of 2 limes

Add the whole pimiento seeds to a spice grinder or coffee grinder. Grind until you have the consistency of coarse ground pepper; set aside.

Add the peppers, onion, scallions, ginger, thyme and garlic to the bowl of a food processor and pulverize. Transfer to a mixing bowl large enough to hold all of the ingredients. Add the ground pimiento, cinnamon, nutmeg, brown sugar, black pepper, soy sauce, vegetable oil and lime juice. Stir to combine. Pour the marinade over your choice of meat and toss to coat well. Cover with plastic wrap and refrigerate overnight.

This marinade is best with pork, chicken or ribs. If you are using chicken, rub the marinade all over as well as under the skin and in the cavities. If you are using pork shoulder score the meat before covering in the marinade.

Cook the meat on an outdoor grill as the fumes from the peppers are very strong.

Note: This should be enough marinade for about 3 pounds of meat.

Yield: Makes 1 1/2 cups

Brown Butter Sauce

This is a nice sauce served over sautéed chicken or fish.

1/2 cup clarified butter
1/4 cup fresh parsley, minced
juice of 2 lemons

If you are making this sauce after sautéing a meat dish, add the clarified butter to the hot skillet and scrape up any renderings left behind. Otherwise heat the clarified butter in a clean skillet until it has turned a light golden brown; about 3 minutes. Immediately remove from heat and stir in the parsley and lemon juice.

Note: Clarified butter doesn't burn like pure butter because you have removed the protein casein. This protein tends to cause the butter to scorch and smoke. Without this component you can cook with it at higher temperatures. This is a great solution when you want that butter flavor but you need to sauté something hotter and for a longer period of time. The smoke point for pure butter is 250 degrees compared to that of clarified butter which is 350 degrees.

To clarify the butter place the desired amount in a saucepan over medium low heat. Watch carefully and heat until just melted. When the butter has melted pour it into a clear glass measuring cup, set it aside to cool and leave it undisturbed. After about 10 minutes you will see the melted butter has separated into 3 layers. The bottom layer will be white and milky, the middle is a clear yellow which is the clarified butter and the top is white foam.

Gently spoon the foam off of the top and carefully pour out the clear yellow butter into a container without disturbing the bottom layer. Discard the white and milky bottom layer.

I always clarify more butter than what is called for in a recipe so I don't run short as it can always be used for another dish. Store any extra clarified butter in the refrigerator. Clarified butter has a longer shelf life than pure butter even when kept at room temperature.

Yield: Serves 4

Cajun Seasoning

2 teaspoons salt
2 teaspoons crushed red pepper
1 tablespoon dried basil
1 tablespoon ground coriander
1/2 cup paprika
1/2 cup garlic powder
1/4 cup onion powder
3 tablespoons black pepper
2 teaspoons cayenne pepper
1/4 cup dried oregano
1/4 cup dried thyme
2 teaspoons ground cumin

Combine all of the ingredients in a medium size bowl and mix well. It will keep for several months if it is kept in a glass container with a tight fitting lid.

Note: This seasoning blend is very versatile. You can sprinkle it on shrimp, fish, chicken, eggs or just about anything that you want to kiss with a little cajun flavor.

Yield: Makes 2 3/4 Cups

Herb Cream Butter Sauce

1/2 cup beef stock
1 1/3 cups heavy cream
salt and pepper
1/2 teaspoon nutmeg
1/2 teaspoon lemon juice
4 tablespoons butter
2 tablespoons fresh parsley, minced
2 tablespoons fresh tarragon, minced

This recipe is best when you have just sautéed meat and you have tasty bits of renderings left behind in the bottom of the skillet.

Over medium high heat add the stock and cook it down quickly while scraping the bottom of the skillet and lifting off any renderings. Cook until it is reduced to about 1/4 cup and slightly clings to a spoon. Reduce the heat to medium low and add the cream; cook it down rapidly while stirring constantly. Watch carefully as it can scald on the bottom very easily. Simmer until it has reduced by half and thickened slightly. Season with salt, pepper, nutmeg and lemon juice. Remove from heat and add the butter by tablespoons until it has melted. Stir in the herbs and spoon the sauce over the meat and serve.

Note: One of my favorite ways to serve this sauce is over fillet mignons or even a simple hamburger patty! It is also good over chicken, fish or vegetables.

Yield: Serves 6

Jalapeño Hot Sauce

3 tablespoons vegetable oil
20 jalapeño peppers, diced
4 cloves garlic, minced
1 medium onion, diced
1/2 teaspoon salt
2 cups water
1 cup white vinegar

Add the oil to a medium size skillet and heat over medium high heat. Add the peppers, garlic, onions and salt. Sauté for 3 to 4 minutes or until soft and translucent, stirring occasionally. Add the water and cook at a low simmer for about 20 minutes. Remove from heat and let cool completely. Once the mixture has cooled add it to a food processor and puree while slowly adding the vinegar. Place the sauce into very clean jars with tight fitting lids. Store in the refrigerator. The sauce will keep for a few months if kept refrigerated.

Yield: Makes 4 cups

Mexican Seasoning

2 tablespoons chile powder
1 1/2 teaspoons garlic powder
1 1/2 teaspoons onion powder
1/2 teaspoon crushed red pepper
1 teaspoon dried oregano
1 teaspoon paprika
1 tablespoon ground cumin
2 teaspoons sea salt
2 teaspoons black pepper

Combine all of the ingredients in a small bowl and mix well.

After browning ground beef or sautéing chicken use 2 tablespoons of the seasoning per 1 pound of meat along with 1/3 cup of water. Add the seasoning and water to the cooked meat, stir and simmer until the water has evaporated.

This also makes a great dry rub to use before cooking chicken, beef or pork.

Yield: Makes 6 tablespoons

Pan Sauces

3 tablespoons olive oil
1/4 cup shallots, finely chopped
1/2 tablespoon garlic, minced
1/2 cup dry white wine
1/2 cup chicken stock
2 tablespoons heavy cream
3 tablespoons cold butter

In a medium skillet over medium high heat (preferably the one used after you have browned or cooked your meat or fish) add the oil and cook until hot. Add the shallots and garlic. Cook for 3 to 4 minutes or just until slightly translucent. Add the wine and bring to a gentle simmer and cook until reduced by half. Add the stock and gently simmer uncovered for about 10 minutes or until liquid is reduced to about 1/4 cup. Reduce heat to low.

Stir in the heavy cream. Add the butter, one tablespoon at a time, stirring until butter is melted after each addition. Sauce should be slightly thickened. Season to taste with salt and pepper if desired. Serve over chicken, fish, pork or beef.

Variations:
Herb-Stir 2 to 3 teaspoons finely chopped fresh herbs like basil, chervil, parsley, oregano or dill into the finished sauce.
Mushroom-Add 1 cup sliced fresh mushrooms to the skillet with the shallots; do not add wine and broth at this point. Cook until tender and golden. Add wine and broth and continue from there as recipe directs.
Bacon and Leek-Add 1/2 cup sliced leeks to the skillet with shallots. Stir 3 slices crumbled, crisp cooked bacon into the finished sauce.
Lemon and Thyme-Stir 2 teaspoons lemon juice and 2 teaspoons fresh thyme into the finished sauce.
Mustard-Stir in 1 tablespoon chopped parsley and 2 teaspoons Dijon mustard into finished sauce.

Yield: Makes 1/4 cup

Rosemary Pesto

1 cup rosemary leaves, stems removed
2 cups parsley leaves, stems removed
3 tablespoons pine nuts, roasted
3 cloves garlic
1/4 cup Parmesan cheese, grated
1/4 teaspoon salt
1/2 cup olive oil

Place the rosemary, parsley, pine nuts, garlic, Parmesan cheese and salt into a food processor. Puree while slowly adding the olive oil. Process until smooth. Use immediately or store in the refrigerator in a covered dish with a layer of olive oil on top to keep it from turning brown. This is a very nice accompaniment to chicken or lamb.

Yield: Serves 6

Scotch Bonnet Pepper Sauce

2 tablespoons olive oil
2 cups carrots, finely chopped
1 medium onion, chopped
2 tablespoons garlic, minced
20 scotch bonnet peppers, cleaned and stemmed
juice of 4 limes
1/2 cup white vinegar
1/2 cup boiled water, cooled
pinch of salt

Heat the olive oil in a medium size skillet over medium heat. When the oil is hot add the carrots and onions. Sauté until the vegetables are slightly soft, about 5 minutes. Add the garlic and cook a few more minutes. Transfer the onion and carrot mixture to a food processor. Add the scotch bonnet peppers, lime juice, vinegar, water and salt. Process until smooth. Transfer back to the skillet and simmer on low heat for 10 minutes. Remove from heat and cool. Spoon into 4 clean (6 ounce) canning jars. Will keep for several months if stored in the refrigerator. Note: I recommend that you wear gloves and process in a well ventilated area.

Yield: Makes 3 cups

Sweet Red Pepper Sauce

You've got to love this sauce! It goes well with fish, chicken or beef. It compliments just about anything that you pair it with. I personally love it with a nice steak or crab cakes.

1/4 cup vegetable oil
1 large onion, chopped
1/2 cup garlic, minced
5 medium red bell peppers, seeded and diced
1 bunch cilantro, finely chopped
1/2 cup honey
1/2 scotch bonnet pepper, seeded and chopped
2 cups barbecue sauce
1/2 cup chicken stock
1/4 cup molasses

Heat the oil in a large skillet over medium high heat. Once the oil is hot add the onions and garlic; sauté until the onions are lightly golden and transculent.

Add the red bell pepper and cilantro, cook for about 10 minutes or until the peppers are tender. Add the remaining ingredients and bring to a gentle boil. Immediately reduce the heat to low and simmer for 30 minutes. Remove the skillet from the heat and set aside to cool.

Transfer the mixture to a blender and puree until very fine. Reheat before serving. You can also make this sauce in advance for convenience. It only gets better on the second day.

Yield: Makes 3 1/2 cups

Thai Chile Pepper Sauce

24 fresh Thai chile peppers
1 cup white wine vinegar
1 teaspoon salt
1 teaspoon sugar
1 canning jar (12 ounces)

Wash the Thai chile peppers and set aside.

In a small saucepan add the vinegar, salt and sugar. Bring to a gentle boil over medium heat while stirring occasionally. Remove from heat and cool for about 5 to 10 minutes.

Add the peppers to the clean jar and pour the vinegar mixture over the peppers while filling to about 1 inch from top.

Cover with a tight fitting lid and store in the refrigerator. Let marinade for about 3 to 4 weeks. The longer the peppers sit the spicier the sauce will become. The sauce will keep for about 6 months if stored in the refrigerator.

Yield: Makes 1 jar (12 ounces)

Zippy Mayonnaise

1 1/2 cups mayonnaise
juice of 1 lime
1 tablespoon Creole mustard
1 tablespoon chipotle peppers in Adobo sauce, mashed into a paste
1 tablespoon roasted garlic, mashed into a paste
2 tablespoons fresh cilantro, finely chopped
salt and pepper to taste

Combine the mayonnaise, lime juice, Creole mustard, chipotle peppers in Adobo sauce, garlic and cilantro in a medium sized bowl and stir well. Add salt and pepper to taste.

Put the Zippy mayonnaise in a squeeze bottle and decoratively dress the mayonnaise over carpaccio, sandwiches, deviled eggs, Mexican dishes or any thing that suits your taste.

Note: See the recipe for Roasted Garlic in the section "Appetizers".

Refrigerate until ready to use.

Yield: Makes 2 Cups

Chateaubriand Sauce

1/2 cup white wine
1 tablespoon shallots, finely chopped
1 1/2 cups beef stock
6 tablespoons butter
2 teaspoons fresh tarragon, minced
juice of 1/2 lemon
1/8 teaspoon pepper

In a skillet over medium high heat bring the wine and shallots to a simmer and cook until reduced to about 1/4 cup. Add the beef stock and reduce again to about 1/2 cup. Remove from heat and add the butter one tablespoon at a time; melting each one as they are added. Add the tarragon, lemon juice and pepper; stir to combine.

Serve hot over beef tenderloin.

Yield: Makes 1 cup

Cocktail Sauce

1 cup ketchup
3 tablespoons prepared horseradish
2 drops Tabasco sauce
1/2 teaspoon Worcestershire sauce
juice of 1 lemon

In a small bowl combine all of the ingredients and mix well. Serve with fresh cold shrimp, crabmeat or oysters.

Keep refrigerated and serve cold.

Yield: Makes 1 1/4 cups

Cranberry Sauce

1 cup water
1 cup sugar
2 tablespoons orange juice
12 ounces fresh cranberries
1 tablespoon orange zest, finely grated

Heat the water and sugar in a medium size saucepan over low heat; stir until the sugar is dissolved. Slowly bring to a gentle boil. Add the orange juice, cranberries and orange zest. Bring back to a gentle boil for 10 minutes while watching it continuously and stirring often. Remove from heat and cool to room temperature. Refrigerate until very cold. This sauce is better made the day before to insure it is congealed, cold and flavors have married.

Yield: Serves 12

Cucumber and Dill Tzatziki

1 cup Greek yogurt, plain
1 cucumber, peeled, seeded and finely diced
1 clove garlic, minced
2 tablespoons fresh dill, finely chopped plus extra for garnish.
salt and pepper

Combine the yogurt, cucumber, garlic and dill in a medium bowl. Season with salt and pepper. Stir to combine.

Garnish with fresh chopped dill. Refrigerate until ready to use.

Yield: Serves 6

Elliot's Tartar Sauce

1 tablespoon shallots, finely minced
2 tablespoons fresh parsley, finely chopped
1 tablespoon fresh dill, finely chopped
1 cup mayonnaise
1 tablespoon capers

Mix all of the ingredients until well blended. Refrigerate until ready to use. Makes 1 1/2 cups.

Yield: Serves 8

Horseradish Cream

1/4 cup whipping heavy cream
1/4 cup prepared horseradish
2 tablespoons vinegar
salt to taste

In a small bowl beat the cream until stiff. Gently stir in the horseradish one tablespoon at a time. Add the vinegar and salt; combine well. Refrigerate until needed.

Yield: Makes 1/2 cup

Mint Pesto

2 cups fresh mint
1 cup fresh basil
1/2 cup Parmesan cheese, grated
1/3 cup pine nuts, toasted
2 cloves garlic
1/3 cup olive oil
salt and pepper

Combine the mint, basil, Parmesan cheese, pine nuts and garlic in the bowl of a food processor. Puree while slowly adding the oil. This pesto is best served with lamb.

Keep refrigerated until ready to use.

Yield: Serves 6

Remoulade Sauce

1 cup mayonnaise
1/4 cup Dijon mustard
2 tablespoons ketchup
2 teaspoons prepared horseradish
1 teaspoon Worcestershire sauce
1 1/2 tablespoons lemon juice
Tabasco sauce to taste
1/2 cup parsley, chopped
1/4 cup green onions, chopped
1/2 cup celery, minced
2 tablespoons capers, drained

Combine all of the ingredients together in a medium bowl. Refrigerate and serve cold. Serve with crab, shrimp or on a seafood salad.

Yield: Makes 2 1/2 cups

White Cream Sauces

Thin:
1 tablespoon butter
1 tablespoon flour
1/2 teaspoon salt
1/8 teaspoon pepper
1 cup whole milk

Medium:
2 tablespoons butter
2 tablespoons flour
1/2 teaspoon salt
1/8 teaspoon pepper
1 cup whole milk

Thick:
1/4 cup butter
1/4 cup flour
3/4 teaspoon salt
1/8 teaspoon pepper
1 cup whole milk

Melt the butter over a medium low heat and slowly add the flour, salt and pepper. Using a whisk stir until it is a smooth paste. Continue to cook for about 2 minutes. Reduce the heat to low and slowly add the milk, stirring constantly until thick and smooth. Add more or less milk if necessary. Watch carefully as it can scald on the bottom very easily. Makes 1 cup.

Variations:
Béchamel: Substitute 1 cup of chicken stock for milk in the thick cream sauce, add a sprinkling of paprika and stir in 1 cup of cream. Serve with chicken, vegetables or veal.
Caper: Add 3 tablespoons of chopped capers and 1 teaspoon of lemon juice to cream sauce. Serve with fish.
Curry: Add 1/2 teaspoon of curry powder to cream sauce. Serve with fish or rice.
Dill: Add 1/2 teaspoon dried dill to cream sauce. Serve with fish, chicken or vegetables.
Mornay: Add 1/2 to 1 cup of Swiss cheese and a pinch of nutmeg to the medium cream sauce. Serve with chicken or vegetables.

Memphis Barbecue

Another fun filled day at the cottage chopping pork shoulders and slicing ribs! Everyone is all smiles in anticipation of the infamous barbecue our "Grill Master" can throw down! If you are fortunate enough to be asked to help work "The Pit" be ready because roll call starts in the wee hours of the morning and it can be a long hot day, but it's worth every minute!

Baked Beans with Molasses

1 pound bacon, cut into 1 inch pieces
1 can (#10 or 109 ounces) baked beans
1 can (17 ounces) baked beans
4 medium green peppers, diced
4 medium onions, diced
2 cups molasses (16 ounces)
1 teaspoon oregano
1/2 cup Worcestershire sauce (4 ounces)
1/2 cup red wine vinegar (4 ounces)
1/4 cup yellow mustard (2 ounces)
1 cup dark brown sugar (8 ounces)
1 cup barbecue sauce (8 ounces)
2 teaspoons celery salt
2 teaspoons lemon pepper
1 tablespoon olive oil
2 teaspoons garlic powder

Preheat oven to 350 degrees.

In a large skillet cook the bacon until just crisp. Drain on paper towels.

In a large and sturdy baking dish (I use a large roasting pan), combine the bacon, baked beans, green peppers and onions. Finish by adding the remaining ingredients and stir to combine.

Bake covered for 1 hour. Remove cover and bake for an additional 30 minutes or until completely heated through.

Serve while hot.

Note: I don't recommend using a disposable aluminum pan for this recipe. I have found the disposable pans aren't strong enough to support the weight.

Yield: Serves 48

Brother Bill's Marinade

9 cups olive oil (72 ounces)
4 1/2 cups soy sauce (36 ounces)
1 1/2 cups Worcestershire sauce (12 ounces)
3/4 cup dry mustard powder (6 ounces)
1/4 cup salt (2 ounces)
1/4 cup ground black pepper (2 ounces)
3 cups red wine vinegar (24 ounces)
2 cups lemon juice (16 ounces)
1/4 cup dried parsley flakes (2 ounces)
12 cloves garlic, mashed

Combine all of the ingredients in a large stock pot.

This marinade can be used for beef, pork or chicken. Marinade for at least 4 hours or overnight if possible.

This recipe makes enough marinade for 3 pork shoulders and 24 slabs of ribs and can be made in advance.

Yield: Serves 48

Kathy's Potato Salad

18 eggs
15 pounds potatoes, mixture of red and white (see note below)
1/4 cup salt (2 ounces)
4 cups celery, chopped
6 cups mayonnaise (48 ounces)
salt and pepper to taste
celery seed to taste
2 disposable aluminum half pans

Place the eggs in a large pot and cover with fresh cold water. Bring the water to a full boil. Once the water is boiling quickly turn off the heat and place a tight fitting lid on the pot and cover for exactly 12 minutes. After the 12 minutes have passed immediately pour off the hot water and run cold water over the eggs to stop the cooking process. Crack and peel the eggs under warm running water. Set the eggs aside.

Wash and peel the potatoes; cut into about 2 1/2 inch pieces. Place the potatoes in a large stock pot filled with enough water to cover and add 1/4 cup of salt. Bring to a full boil over high heat. Boil for about 20 minutes or until the potatoes are fork tender.

Once the potatoes are tender immediately drain them in a colander over the sink. DO NOT rinse the potatoes. Place the colander of potatoes on a clean kitchen towel and set aside to cool.

Meanwhile chop the boiled eggs and set aside.

When the potatoes have cooled completely divide them evenly between the 2 disposable aluminum half pans along with the chopped eggs, celery and mayonnaise. Sprinkle with generous amounts of salt, pepper and celery seed to taste. Stir to combine and taste for seasonings.

Note: Yukon Gold is a good choice of potatoes to use as they hold up well where as Russet Potatoes do not.

Yield: Serves 48

Kick Butt Hot Sauce

Let me introduce you to the "Dancing Bear Barbecue" team. As you can see we take our barbecue very seriously!

3 medium onions, minced
9 cups ketchup (72 ounces)
6 tablespoons Worcestershire sauce (3 ounces)
3 tablespoons chili powder
2 tablespoons cayenne pepper
2 1/4 cups sugar (18 ounces)
1 tablespoon garlic salt
1 1/2 cups tarragon vinegar (12 ounces)

Combine all of the ingredients together in a stock pot and bring to a gentle boil. Once the sauce is boiling immediately reduce the heat to low and cook while stirring often. Cook for 1 hour.

This can be made in advance. Cool and refrigerate until ready to use. Serve over ribs or pork shoulder. It can be served hot or cold.

Yield: Serves 48

Macaroni Salad (For a Crowd)

2 pounds elbow macaroni (32 ounces)
2 1/2 cups celery, chopped
2 1/2 cups onions, chopped
8 eggs, hard boiled and peeled
5 cups mayonnaise (40 ounces)
salt and pepper to taste

According to my Mother-in-law Ruthie, the trick to this recipe is for all of the ingredients to be dry so the mayonnaise sticks to the pasta, celery and onions.

Cook the macaroni according to the package directions for al dente. Immediately remove from heat and drain the pasta in a colander and rinse under cold water to stop the cooking process. Leave the macaroni in the colander sitting on a clean dish towel and refrigerate uncovered along with the celery, onions and eggs. Refrigerate overnight so they become cold and dry.

Chop the eggs on the morning of the day you are serving the salad. Place all of the ingredients in a very large bowl and combine well. Refrigerate again until ready to serve. Stir once again just before serving and adjust the salt and pepper if needed. You may need to add more mayonnaise at this point if the pasta seems a little dry.

Serve cold.

Yield: Serves 24

Memphis Red Rub

2 tablespoons celery seed
1 tablespoon oregano
1 tablespoon thyme
1 tablespoon dry mustard
1 tablespoon ground coriander
2 tablespoons allspice
1/2 cup paprika (4 ounces)
1/2 cup salt (4 ounces)
1/2 cup brown sugar (4 ounces)
1/2 cup garlic powder (4 ounces)
6 tablespoons onion powder (3 ounces)
1/4 cup chili powder (2 ounces)
1 tablespoon black pepper
1 teaspoon cumin
1/2 teaspoon cayenne pepper

Mix all of the ingredients into a medium size bowl and combine well. This is a great dry rub to use before cooking and before serving any barbecued meat. If it is kept in a jar with a tight fitting lid it will stay fresh for several months. This is enough rub for 3 pork shoulders and 24 racks of ribs.

Yield: Makes 3 Cups

Mild Barbecue Sauce

1/4 cup vegetable oil (2 ounces)
2 medium onions, finely minced
3 cloves garlic, minced
4 1/2 cups ketchup (36 ounces)
3/4 cup brown sugar (6 ounces)
3/4 cup molasses (6 ounces)
1/2 cup Jack Daniel's Whiskey (4 ounces)
1/2 cup apple cider vinegar (4 ounces)
1 1/2 teaspoons dry mustard powder
6 drops Tabasco sauce

In a large stock pot add the vegetable oil and heat over medium high heat until hot. Add the onions and garlic, sauté until they are soft and translucent. Stir in the remaining ingredients. Bring to a gentle boil and immediately reduce the heat to low. Simmer uncovered for 1 hour while stirring occasionally. This can be made in advance. Cool and refrigerate until ready to use.

Serve over pulled pork barbecue or ribs. Serve hot or cold.

Yield: Serves 48

Shelby's Cobbler (For a Crowd)

2 quarts (8 cups or 64 ounces) berries, apples, peaches or fruit of choice (if using apples add a little cinnamon to the sugar)
4 1/2 cups sugar (36 ounces), divided
4 cups flour (32 ounces)
4 teaspoons baking powder
1 cup butter, melted
2 1/2 cups whole milk (20 ounces)
2 aluminum disposable half pans (holds 120 ounces each)
1 gallon vanilla ice cream

Preheat oven to 350 degrees.

Prepare the pans with cooking spray and set them aside.

Wash the fruit and slice it if necessary. Place the fruit in a very large bowl and sweeten it with 1/2 cup of the sugar. Stir the fruit gently and set it aside. In a large bowl mix together the flour, baking powder and 4 cups of sugar; combine well. Add the melted butter and milk, mix on low to medium low speed with an electric mixer. Do not over mix the batter as it will get tough. Pour the batter into the prepared half pans, dividing evenly between the two. Place the sweetened fruit on top of the batter.

Bake for 1 hour and 15 minutes or until it is golden brown and bubbly in the center. Remove from the oven and let it cool. It can be served warm or at room temperature. It's always better with a scoop of vanilla ice cream!

Note: Do not overfill the baking pans. I also suggest placing a foil lined baking sheet under the pans in order to catch any over flow.

Yield: Serves 12 to 16

Sopping Sauce

This southern girl taught her beau many things about pork barbecue and many things he learned on his own. However, the most important lesson I taught him was how to tell when the barbecue was cooked through and ready to serve. It's not particularly scientific but it works like a charm every time. You simply start the pork shoulders very early in the morning, crack a new bottle of Jack Daniels, sip on it all day with your co-chefs while tending to the smoker. When the bottle is empty the pork is done! It's a tried and true method. Sometimes we just don't need to make things harder than they need to be!

6 cups water (48 ounces)
3 cups white vinegar (24 ounces)
3 cups butter (24 ounces)
1 1/2 cups sugar (12 ounces)
2 tablespoons black pepper
1/4 cup salt (2 ounces)
1 tablespoon cayenne pepper
3/4 cup yellow prepared mustard (6 ounces)
3 large lemons, sliced
6 medium onions, coarsely chopped
1 1/2 cups Worcestershire sauce (12 ounces)

This is enough sauce for 3 pork shoulders and 24 slabs of ribs. Combine all of the ingredients in a large pot. Bring to a boil over medium high heat. Reduce the heat to low and simmer for 20 minutes. If the sauce is not being used immediately cool and refrigerate. Can be made in advance.

Note: Sopping sauce is just a glorified name for a basting sauce. Simply brush the sopping sauce over the pork and ribs periodically while they are in the smoker.

Yield: Makes about 15 cups

Southern Banana Pudding (For a Crowd)

4 boxes vanilla wafer cookies (11 ounces each)
1 gallon whole milk
8 boxes vanilla pudding, cook and serve, not instant (24 ounces)
12 bananas, ripe and sliced about 1/4 inch thick
2 aluminum disposable half pans (holds 120 ounces each)

Line the bottom and sides of each aluminum half pan with the vanilla wafers and set aside.

In a large stockpot over medium heat add the milk. Slowly add the pudding mix while whisking constantly. Watch carefully as it will burn on the bottom very easily. Bring the mixture to a low boil and continue to stir constantly until the pudding has thickened. Once it has thickened remove from heat.

In the wafer lined pan layer in the ingredients while the pudding is still warm. Alternately layer in the pudding, bananas and more wafers. Finishing with wafers garnishing the top of the pudding.

Set aside to cool and refrigerate or serve warm. I particularly like my banana pudding really cold. This is the perfect dessert to make a day in advance.

Yield: Serves 32

Southern Slaw (For a Crowd)

4 heads of cabbage, shredded
12 large carrots, grated
2 cups sugar (16 ounces)
1/2 cup prepared yellow mustard (4 ounces)
1 cup white vinegar (8 ounces)
4 teaspoons salt
1 1/2 cups vegetable oil (12 ounces)

Note: If you can buy the pre-shredded slaw mix with the carrots in it you can omit the above cabbage and carrots. You will need about 5 pounds.

Place the shredded cabbage and grated carrots in an extra large bowl and set aside. In a large mixing bowl add the sugar, mustard, vinegar, salt and oil; whisk together. Pour over the cabbage and carrots, gently toss to combine.

Cover with plastic wrap and refrigerate. Let marinade for several hours or overnight before serving.

Serve cold.

Yield: Serves 48

Sunday Grits (For a Crowd)

We call these "Sunday Grits" because they are all dressed up for Church with their cheese and garlic on!

4 1/2 quarts water
4 teaspoons salt
4 cups uncooked grits, not instant (32 ounces)
2 cups butter (16 ounces)
1/4 cup garlic, minced (2 ounces)
6 cups cheddar cheese, grated (48 ounces)
2 cups whole milk (16 ounces)
8 eggs, beaten and room temperature

Preheat oven to 350 degrees.

Prepare a large and sturdy baking dish with cooking spray and set aside.

Bring the water and salt to a boil in a large stock pot. Slowly add in the grits. Reduce the heat to medium low and stir. Cook for 15 minutes or until thickened, stirring constantly. Add the butter, garlic and cheese; continue to stir constantly until the cheese is melted. Turn off the heat and cool slightly. Warm the milk in the microwave (NOT HOT). Add the room temperature eggs to a medium size bowl and beat well. Slowly add the warm milk to the eggs while whisking constantly. Slowly add the milk and egg mixture to the grits and continue to stir until well combined.

Pour into the prepared sturdy 4 quart baking dish and bake for 1 hour or until heated through completely.

Note: I don't recommend using a disposable aluminum pan for this recipe. I have found the disposable pans aren't strong enough to support the weight.

Yield: Serves 48

Shopping List for Memphis Barbecue

Southern Barbecue for 48 people

Menu:
Baked Beans with Molasses
Brother Bill's Marianade
Kathy's Potato Salad
Kick Butt Hot Sauce
Macaroni Salad (For a Crowd)
Memphis Red Rub
Mild Barbecue Sauce
Shelby's Cobbler (For a Crowd)
Sopping Sauce
Southern Banana Pudding (For a Crowd)
Southern Slaw (For a Crowd)
Sunday Grits (For a Crowd)

Herbs and Spices:
1 ounce allspice
2 ounces cayenne pepper
1 ounce celery salt
2 ounces celery seed
2 ounces chili powder
1 ounce ground coriander
1 ounce ground cumin
6 ounces garlic powder
1 ounce garlic salt
1 ounce lemon pepper
8 ounces dry mustard powder
4 ounces onion powder
1 ounce oregano
4 ounces paprika
2 ounces dried parsley flakes
8 ounces black pepper
16 ounces salt
1 ounce thyme

Frozen:
1 gallon vanilla ice cream

Meat:
1 pound bacon
3 pork shoulders
24 racks baby back ribs

Perishables:
48 ounces butter
48 ounces cheddar cheese, grated
36 eggs
2 gallons whole milk

Non-Perishables:
126 ounces baked beans
1 ounce baking powder
8 ounces barbecue sauce
4 boxes vanilla wafer cookies
32 ounces flour
32 ounces grits, uncooked (not instant)
128 ounces ketchup
16 ounces lemon juice
2 pounds elbow macaroni
96 ounces mayonnaise
32 ounces molasses
12 ounces yellow mustard
72 ounces olive oil
4 boxes vanilla pudding, cook and serve (not instant)
36 ounces soy sauce
84 ounces sugar
24 ounces dark brown sugar
1 ounce Tabasco sauce
4 ounces apple cider vinegar
28 ounces red wine vinegar
12 ounces tarragon vinegar
32 ounces white vinegar
4 ounces Jack Daniel's Whiskey
32 ounces Worcestershire sauce
16 ounces vegetable oil

Produce:
2 quarts (8 cups or 64 ounces) berries, apples or peaches
12 bananas, ripe
2 bunches celery
24 cloves garlic
3 large lemons
18 medium onions
4 medium green peppers
15 pounds potatoes (Yukon Gold)
5 pounds pre-shredded slaw mix or 4 heads of cabbage and 12 large carrots

Cooking Supplies:
12 aluminum disposable pans, half size
12 aluminum disposable pans, full size

Soups and Stews

LEE
33

Chicken and Dumplings

3 to 4 pounds chicken breast and thighs, skinless
8 cups chicken stock, divided
3 medium carrots, diced
3 stalks celery, chopped
1 teaspoon dried thyme
salt and pepper
2 tablespoons fresh parsley, chopped
2 teaspoons poultry seasoning
3/4 cup whole milk, divided
1/8 teaspoon onion powder
1/8 teaspoon garlic powder
1/8 teaspoon paprika
1/4 cup plus 2 tablespoons flour
Dumplings (see recipe in section "Breads")

Wash the chicken and place it in a large stock pot with 7 & 1/4 cups of the chicken stock. Add the carrots, celery, thyme, salt, pepper, parsley and poultry seasoning. Bring to a gentle boil, reduce heat and simmer on low uncovered for about 40 minutes. Skim any fat off of the top as needed. Cook until the chicken is tender and cooked through with no signs of pink. Remove the chicken from the stock and cool enough to remove the meat from the bones. Discard the bones and return the meat back to the pot. Cover and simmer on low to keep warm.

Make the thickening mixture by adding 3/4 cup of the stock to a medium size saucepan along with 1/3 cup of milk, onion powder, garlic powder and paprika. Bring to a gentle boil while stirring constantly for about two minutes. Immediately reduce the heat to a low simmer. In a separate bowl make a thickening slurry by whisking together 1/3 cup of milk and the flour, mix until completely combined. Add the slurry mixture to the saucepan of milk and stock; stir to combine well. Continue cooking until the mixture thickens. Add the thickened mixture to the chicken and broth in the large stock pot. Stir to combine and simmer gently for about 30 minutes.

Meanwhile make the dumplings according to the recipe (see recipe in section "Breads"). Drop the dumplings carefully into the chicken and broth. Occasionally ladle the hot liquid over the dumplings. Simmer for about 10 minutes uncovered and 10 minutes covered or until the dumplings are done in the middle.

Serve hot.

Yield: Serves 8 to 10

Clam Chowder

1/2 pound bacon, cut into 1 inch pieces for garnish
1 cup onion, finely chopped
2 stalks celery, chopped
salt and pepper to taste
1 tablespoon garlic, minced
1/4 cup all purpose flour
6 cups chicken stock
4 cups potatoes, peeled and diced
3 cups fresh clams (steamed and shucked), cut into small pieces
1 1/2 cups half and half
2 tablespoons butter
2 teaspoons fresh thyme, finely chopped
pinch cayenne pepper
2 tablespoons fresh parsley, chopped

In a large stock pot over medium high heat cook the bacon until crisp. Remove the bacon and drain on paper towels. Set aside to cool.

Pour off all but 1/4 cup of the bacon grease from the pot. Add the onions and celery. Season with salt and pepper. Cook until the onions and celery are soft. Add the garlic and cook for 2 to 3 more minutes. Sprinkle in the flour and stir into the vegetables, cook for 3 to 4 minutes. Slowly add the stock while stirring constantly. Once the mixture is blended add the potatoes, cover and bring to a gentle boil. Reduce the heat to low and simmer for 12 to 15 minutes or until the potatoes are tender. Add the clams, cover and gently simmer for 5 to 6 minutes. Do not over cook once the clams are added as they will get tough.

Stir in the half and half, butter, thyme and cayenne pepper. Add more salt and pepper if needed. Heat on low until thoroughly hot. Ladle into bowls and garnish with a sprinkle of parsley and the bacon.

Serve hot.

Yield: Serves 6 to 8

Potato and Leek Soup

6 leeks, white part only
3 tablespoons butter
1/2 pound bacon, cut into 1 inch slices
1 medium onion, chopped
3 cloves garlic, minced
1/2 cup dry white wine
8 cups chicken stock
4 medium russet potatoes, peeled and cut into 1/8's
1 teaspoon salt
1/2 teaspoon pepper
1 tablespoon fresh thyme
1 cup heavy cream
1/2 bunch green onions, chopped for garnish

Trim the green part off of the leeks. Half the white part of the leeks lengthwise being careful not to cut to the very end so the leek will stay together. Fan out the leeks and wash thoroughly under cold running water to rid the leek of any sand and dirt. Trim off the bottom and slice into 1/4 inch pieces crosswise and set aside.

In a large stock pot over medium high heat melt the butter and add the bacon. Cook until the fat is rendered from the bacon and it is cooked through. Add the chopped leeks, onions and garlic. Cook until wilted, about 5 minutes. Add the wine and bring to a simmer for about 3 minutes. Add the chicken stock, potatoes, salt and pepper; bring to a gentle boil. Reduce the heat and cook for about 20 minutes or until the potatoes are tender. Add the thyme. Remove from heat and let cool slightly.

Carefully puree the warm soup with an immersion blender. Stir in the heavy cream and adjust the seasonings if necessary. Heat on medium low heat until hot throughout. Garnish with green onions. Serve hot.

Yield: Serves 8 to 10

Red Conch Chowder

1 pound fresh conch, pounded and minced
1/4 cup vegetable oil
1 medium green pepper, seeded and finely chopped
1 medium red pepper, seeded and finely chopped
1 medium onion, finely chopped
3 stalks celery, finely chopped
1 medium carrot, finely chopped
1/2 scotch bonnet pepper, seeded and minced
3 tablespoons tomato paste
2 tablespoons paprika
12 cups chicken stock
2 medium potatoes, peeled and diced
1 tablespoon fresh thyme, finely chopped
1 tablespoon fresh basil, finely chopped
salt and pepper to taste

Place the conch between two pieces of wax paper and pound it until it is about 1/4 inch thick. Mince into small pieces and set aside.

In a large stock pot add the vegetable oil and heat on medium high heat. Once the oil is hot add the peppers, onions, celery, carrots and scotch bonnet pepper. Cook until the vegetables are soft, about 5 or 6 minutes.

Add the conch, tomato paste, paprika and chicken stock. Bring to a gentle boil and immediately reduce the heat to low. Cover and simmer for 30 minutes. Add the potatoes, thyme and basil. Continue to simmer on low for about 15 minutes or until the potatoes are fork tender.

Add salt and pepper to taste. Serve hot.

Yield: Serves 10 to 12

Beef Broth

4 pounds beef shanks, cut up
12 cups water
3 stalks celery, cut into 1 inch pieces
2 carrots, cut into 1 inch pieces
2 medium onions, quartered
3 cloves garlic, mashed
2 bay leaves
1 teaspoon salt
1 teaspoon pepper

Preheat oven to 400 degrees.

Place beef shanks in a 13x9x2 inch baking dish. Bake for 20 to 25 minutes or until the beef shanks are browned.

Place the browned beef shanks and drippings in a large stock pot; add the remaining ingredients. Cover and bring to a boil, immediately reduce the heat to very low and simmer for 2 hours. Carefully strain the broth through a fine sieve into a heat proof pot or bowl. Discard the beef shanks and vegetables while reserving the broth. Bring to room temperature, cover and refrigerate until chilled thoroughly. Skim and discard solidified fat from the top of the broth. Refrigerate the broth in a tightly covered container up to 3 days or freeze in an airtight container for 3 months.

Yield: Makes 3 Quarts

Beef Stew

4 cups beef stock, divided
1 package Lipton Onion Soup Mix
2 cups flour, seasoned with salt and pepper
2 1/2 pounds lean stew meat, cubed
1/4 cup vegetable oil
2 stalks celery, cut into 1 inch pieces
1 large onion, roughly chopped
3 tablespoons flour
1/2 cup red wine
4 sprigs fresh thyme
1 large bay leaf
2 stalks carrots, peeled and cut into 1 inch pieces
4 large potatoes, peeled and cut into 2 inch pieces

Mix 1 cup of the beef stock and the package of Lipton Onion Soup Mix in a microwaveable bowl; heat enough to combine and set aside.

Place the flour in a large shallow dish and season with salt and pepper. Pat the meat dry with paper towels and place it in the flour; toss to coat well.

Pour the oil in a stock pot and heat over medium to medium high heat. When the oil is hot add the meat to brown on all sides. You may need to brown the meat in batches. If the meat is crowded in the pot it will steam and not brown properly. Once the meat is brown transfer it to a platter and set aside.

With the stock pot on medium heat, add the celery and onions. Cook until soft and translucent, about 5 minutes. Stir in the 3 tablespoons of flour, one spoonful at a time and cook for an additional 3 minutes or until the flour has a light brown color. Add the red wine to the pot and stir, cook until reduced by half. Place the meat back into the stock pot. Add the onion soup mixture. Add enough stock to the pot to cover all of the ingredients and a little more. Add the thyme and bay leaf. Bring to a gentle boil and immediately reduce the heat to very low and simmer while covered for 3 1/2 to 4 hours or until the meat is fork tender. Occasionally skim off any fat that floats to the surface. During the last 45 minutes of cooking add the carrots and potatoes. Continue cooking until the carrots and potatoes are fork tender, about 15 to 20 minutes. Remove the thyme sprigs and bay leaf before serving.

Serve while hot.

Yield: Serves 4 to 6

Brussels Sprouts and Kielbasa Soup

3 tablespoons olive oil
1 pound Kielbasa sausage, sliced into 1/2 inch pieces
1 medium onion, finely chopped
1 tablespoon garlic, minced
14 ounces Brussels sprouts, coarsely chopped
8 cups chicken stock
1/2 teaspoon salt
1/2 teaspoon pepper
1 can (15 ounces) cannelloni beans

Heat the olive oil in a large stock pot over medium high heat. When the olive oil is hot add the Kielbasa and brown until the fat is rendered out, turning often. Add the chopped onions and sauté until translucent. Add the garlic and cook 1 minute longer. Add the Brussels sprouts to the Kielbasa and onion mixture. Cook until the sprouts are wilted, stirring often. Add the chicken stock, salt and pepper. Bring to a boil and immediately reduce the heat to a low simmer. Cover and let simmer for 20 minutes. Add the beans and simmer for another 10 minutes. Serve hot.

Yield: Serves 8 to 10

Chicken Broth

6 pounds chicken, white and dark meat
12 cups water
3 stalks celery, cut into 1 inch pieces
2 carrots, cut into 1 inch pieces
2 medium onions, quartered
1 bay leaf
1 teaspoon salt
1 teaspoon pepper
1 teaspoon dried thyme
1/2 teaspoon poultry seasoning

Combine all of the ingredients in a large stock pot. Bring to a boil over medium high heat. Reduce the heat to low, cover and simmer for 2 hours. Carefully strain the broth through a fine sieve into a heat proof pot or bowl while reserving the chicken and vegetables for other uses if desired. Bring to room temperature, cover and refrigerate.

Once the broth is totally chilled skim the solidified fat off of the top and discard. Refrigerate in a tightly sealed container up to 3 days or freeze in an airtight container up to 3 months.

Yield: Makes 3 quarts

Cream of Broccoli

1 1/2 pounds fresh broccoli, chopped
1/2 cup onions, chopped
2 tablespoons butter
1 cup potatoes, peeled and diced
3 1/2 cups chicken stock
1/2 teaspoon salt
1 cup half and half
1/8 teaspoon ground nutmeg
salt and pepper to taste

Boil the broccoli in salted boiling water for 3 minutes. Drain well in a colander and set aside.

In a stock pot over medium high heat sauté the onions in the butter for 5 minutes or until soft and translucent. Add the potatoes, stock and salt. Bring to a gentle boil, immediately reduce the heat and simmer for 15 minutes. Add the broccoli and simmer 5 minutes longer or until the potatoes are tender. With an immersion blender puree the soup until you have the desired consistently. Add the half and half and nutmeg. Bring back to a gentle boil and reduce heat to low. Season with salt and pepper.

Serve hot.

Yield: Serves 6 to 8

Kale and Potato Soup

2 leeks, white part only
1/4 cup olive oil
1 medium onion, chopped
3 garlic cloves, minced
16 ounces kale, tough stems removed and coarsely chopped
3 potatoes, unpeeled and diced
8 cups chicken stock
1 teaspoon salt
1 1/2 teaspoons pepper

Trim the green part off of the leeks. Half the white part of the leeks lengthwise being careful not to cut to the very end so the leek will stay together. Fan out the leeks and wash thoroughly under cold running water to rid the leek of any sand and dirt. Trim off the bottom and slice into 1/2 inch pieces crosswise and set aside.

Heat the olive oil in a large stock pot over medium high heat. Once the oil is hot add the chopped onions, leeks and garlic. Cook until the onions and leeks are translucent and soft, about 10 minutes; stirring often. Add the kale and sauté until wilted. Add the diced potatoes, chicken stock, salt and pepper. Bring to a gentle boil and immediately reduce the heat to low. Cook for about 20 minutes or until the kale has softened and the potatoes are fork tender.

Check seasonings, add salt and pepper if needed.

Serve hot.

Yield: Serves 8

Mexican Tortilla Soup

3 tablespoons vegetable oil
2 stalks celery, chopped
1 medium onion, diced
1 medium red pepper, seeded and diced
3 garlic cloves, finely chopped
1/2 jalapeño pepper, seeded and chopped
6 cups chicken stock, divided
1 1/2 tablespoons ground cumin
1 1/2 cups chicken, cooked and shredded
1/2 cup cilantro, chopped
salt and pepper to taste
1 avocado, diced
1 package corn tortilla strips
1/2 cup Monterey Jack cheese, shredded
1/2 cup cheddar cheese, shredded
1 lime, cut into wedges for garnish

Add the oil to a large stock pot over medium high heat. When the oil is hot add the celery, onion and red pepper; sauté until the onions are translucent and vegetables are tender.

Add the garlic and jalapeño pepper; cook for one minute while stirring constantly. Deglaze the pan with 1/2 cup of the chicken stock, scraping any renderings off of the bottom of the pot. Add the remaining stock and bring to a gentle boil. Add the cumin and lower the heat; simmer for about 20 minutes.

Add the chicken, cilantro, salt and pepper. Cover and simmer for an additional 10 minutes.

Just before serving preheat oven to 350 degrees.

Ladle the soup into oven proof bowls, top with avocados, corn tortilla strips and shredded cheese. Place the oven proof bowls on a baking sheet, bake in the oven until the cheese is melted. Garnish with the lime wedges.

Yield: Serves 6

Roasted Garlic Soup

This is one of Bill's favorites. I can picture his face while enjoying this soup, oh the look of satisfaction! No one loves garlic more than he does!

3 tablespoons olive oil
1 cup shallots, chopped
1 cup Roasted Garlic cloves (see recipe in section "Appetizers")
1/2 cup garlic cloves, raw and peeled
5 cups chicken stock
2 cups heavy cream
2 teaspoons fresh marjoram, minced
salt and pepper to taste
1 tablespoon cornstarch
3 tablespoons water
Roasted Garlic Croutons (see recipe in section "Salads and Dressings")
1 bunch green onions, chopped for garnish

Add the olive oil to a large stock pot and heat over medium high heat. Once the oil is hot add the shallots and cook very quickly until lightly brown and tender.

Add the Roasted Garlic and raw garlic, sauté for about 3 minutes. Add the chicken stock, heavy cream and marjoram. Bring to a gentle boil and immediately lower the heat to a simmer for approximately 20 minutes, stirring occasionally. Remove from heat and let cool slightly.

Puree with an immersion blender until you have a smooth consistency. Warm again by bringing the soup to a gentle boil and immediately lower the heat to a simmer. Taste and adjust the seasonings with salt and pepper according to taste.

To thicken the soup dissolve 1 tablespoon of cornstarch with 3 tablespoons of water in a small cup or bowl. Add the cornstarch mixture to the soup, teaspoon by teaspoon while heating and stirring until you have the right consistency. It should resemble the thickness of potato soup. Serve hot with Roasted Garlic Croutons and greens onions for garnish.

Yield: Serves 6

Roasted Red Pepper and Tomato Basil Soup

12 tomatoes, cored and quartered
olive oil, as needed
4 red bell peppers, seeded and quartered
1 yellow onion, cut into wedges
1/2 bulb garlic, divided and skin removed
6 cups chicken stock
1 medium carrot, peeled and diced
1/8 teaspoon paprika
1/8 teaspoon cayenne pepper
2 tablespoons fresh oregano, minced
3 tablespoons fresh basil, minced
salt and pepper to taste
1/4 cup heavy cream
Garnishes: sour cream, basil leaves and Roasted Garlic Croutons (see recipe in section "Salads and Dressings")

Preheat oven to 375 degrees.

Place the tomatoes on a baking sheet. Toss lightly with olive oil. Turn the tomatoes skin side down. Place the red peppers, onions and garlic on a second baking sheet. Toss lightly with olive oil. Turn the peppers skin side down. Roast the tomatoes and vegetables for 1 hour.

Heat the chicken stock over medium high heat in a stock pot. Add the carrots, roasted tomatoes and vegetables, paprika, cayenne pepper, oregano, basil, salt and pepper. Bring to a gentle boil and simmer on low heat for 10 minutes.

Using an immersion blender carefully puree to a fine smooth consistency. Add the cream and bring back to a slow simmer and cook for an additional 30 to 45 minutes. Adjust seasonings if necessary.

Garnish with a dollop of sour cream, basil and Roasted Garlic Croutons.

Yield: Serves 8

Rustic Country Chicken Soup

1/4 cup plus 2 tablespoons vegetable oil, divided
4 cups onions, chopped and divided
4 cups celery, chopped and divided
4 cups carrots, chopped and divided
1 chicken (4 to 6 pounds) cut into pieces with skin and bones
1 bouquet of 5 stems fresh parsley and 3 sprigs of fresh thyme tied together
2 teaspoons whole peppercorns
1 large bay leaf
2 1/2 teaspoons salt
1 package fine egg noodles, cooked according to package directions for al dente
1/2 tablespoon fresh dill, chopped
1 tablespoon fresh parsley, chopped

Heat 3 tablespoons of the oil in a large stock pot over medium high heat. Add one half of the onions, celery and carrots. Cook stirring often until the onions are golden, about 8 to 10 minutes.

Add the chicken and enough cold water to cover by one inch. Bring to a boil over high heat. Add the bouquet of parsley and thyme, peppercorns, bay leaf and salt. Reduce the heat to low and cover partially. Simmer until the chicken is cooked through (no pink) for about 40 minutes, while skimming off any foam that rises to the surface. Remove the chicken from the pot, setting it aside to cool slightly. Meanwhile keep the broth simmering and remove the meat from the bones and tear into small bite size pieces. Return the skin and bones to the pot and cook for one hour while continuing to remove any foam or fat that rises to the top.

Carefully strain the broth, bones, skin and vegetables through a fine mesh sieve into a large heat proof bowl, reserving all of the broth. Discard the vegetable, bone and skin mixture. Add the remaining 3 tablespoons of oil to the stock pot and heat on medium high heat. Once the oil is hot add the second half of onions, carrots and celery; cook stirring often until the vegetables are soft and translucent, about 8 to10 minutes. Add the broth back to the pot and bring to a boil over medium high heat. Reduce the heat to low. Cover partially and simmer until the vegetables are tender, about 15 minutes. When the vegetables are tender add the chicken to the broth and heat through. Check seasonings. Ladle soup over cooked egg noodles in warm bowls and sprinkle with fresh dill and parsley for garnish.

Yield: Serves 8

Spicy Black Bean Soup

This recipe is from Lantana's restaurant in the Cayman Islands. I believe we were two of their first customers when they opened and two of their last before they closed. Many of our favorite dishes came from their tiny cookbook that they shared. It was a great restaurant that we remember fondly. They left behind some wonderful recipes that we continue to savor to this day.

1/2 pound bacon, cut into 1 inch pieces
1 medium onion, finely minced
1 stalk celery, finely minced
1 medium carrot, finely minced
2 tablespoons garlic, finely minced
1/2 scotch bonnet pepper, finely minced
4 cups dry black beans, soaked overnight in just enough water to cover
10 cups chicken stock
2 tablespoons ground cumin
salt and pepper to taste
1 small bunch cilantro, finely chopped
Garnish:
1 cup sour cream
1 bunch green onions, chopped

In a large stock pot over medium high heat cook the bacon until the fat has rendered out. Add the onions, celery, carrots, garlic and scotch bonnet pepper. Cook over medium heat until the vegetables are soft and transculent, about 5 to 6 minutes.

Add the beans (and the water in which they were soaked in), chicken stock and cumin to the cooked vegetables. Bring to a gentle boil, reduce the heat and simmer until the beans are extremely soft. Stir frequently as the beans will stick to the bottom of the pot and burn easily.

Add salt and pepper to taste and lastly add the cilantro. Let cool slightly. Puree the soup with an immersion blender while leaving it a bit chunky.

Gently heat the soup again until thoroughly hot, stirring often. Serve hot and garnish with sour cream and chopped green onions.

Yield: Serves 8

Sweet Corn and Ham Chowder

1/2 cup butter
1/2 cup flour
4 cups whole milk
1 teaspoon salt
1/8 teaspoon pepper
1/2 pound bacon, cut into 1 inch pieces
2 stalks celery, diced
1 medium onion, diced
1/2 medium red bell pepper, seeded and diced
1/2 jalapeño pepper seeded and diced
3 cups chicken stock
2 potatoes, peeled and diced
1 1/2 cups cooked ham, diced
3/4 cup fresh or frozen corn

In a large stock pot melt the butter over medium heat. When the foam subsides slowly add the flour while whisking constantly to form a smooth paste, cook for about 3 minutes. Slowly add the milk and continue to whisk constantly. Add the salt and pepper; stir to combine. Cook at a low simmer for about 10 minutes. Remove from heat and set aside.

In a medium skillet cook the bacon until light brown and crisp. Remove the bacon with a slotted spoon and drain on paper towels, set aside. Drain off all but 3 tablespoons of the bacon grease. Add the celery, onions, red pepper and jalapeño. Cook for about 10 minutes, stirring frequently. Add the cooked bacon and vegetable mixture to the milk broth in the stock pot; stir to combine.

Add the chicken stock, potatoes, ham and corn to the stock pot and bring to a gentle boil; stirring often. Immediately reduce the heat to low and cook for 15 minutes or until the potatoes are fork tender, stirring frequently to prevent the soup from scalding on the bottom. Taste and adjust the seasonings with salt and pepper if necessary.

Yield: Serves 8

Vegetable Soup

1/4 cup vegetable oil
2 garlic cloves, minced
1 medium onion, chopped
3 leeks, white part only and sliced into 1/2 inch pieces
8 cups chicken stock
2 tablespoons tomato paste
1/4 cup fresh parsley, chopped
1 tablespoon basil, thinly sliced
1/2 teaspoon dried oregano
2 stalks celery, chopped
2 medium carrots, diced
1 can (28 ounces) chopped tomatoes
1 can (15 ounces) kidney beans
1 can (15 ounces) cannelloni beans
1 large potato, peeled and diced
8 ounces frozen green beans
8 ounces frozen lima beans
6 ounces fresh spinach
salt and pepper to taste
3/4 cup Parmesan cheese, grated

Heat the oil in a very large stock pot over medium high heat. Once the oil is hot add the garlic, onions and leeks. Cook for about 10 minutes or until translucent and soft; stirring often. Add the stock, tomato paste, parsley, basil, oregano, celery, carrots and tomatoes with their juices. Bring to a gentle boil and immediately reduce the heat to low and simmer for 35 minutes or until the vegetables are tender. Add the kidney beans, cannelloni beans, potatoes, green beans, lima beans and spinach. Salt and pepper to taste. Bring back to a low simmer and cook for 20 minutes or until the potatoes are fork tender.

Ladle the soup into warm bowls and serve with Parmesan cheese sprinkled on top.

Note: This soup freezes well. I tend to keep it on hand at all times. Also if you are unsure on how to clean leeks see the directions given in the recipe for "Potato and Leek Soup" in this section.

Yield: Serves 10 to 12

Louisiana Gumbo

A Yankee at the Hunting Camp

Louisiana Gumbo is a melody of ingredients that can change according to what is available that particular day at the market or by hunting and fishing, not to mention at the least by who's cooking it! Keep in mind what God grows in those Louisiana swamps, like alligator, crocodile, snakes, all kinds of bottom eating fish, frogs and many odd land creatures are not valued by all.

The first time my Yankee of a husband Bill, went to the Bayou State to meet my Grandmother Maw-Maw, I warned him about a couple of issues. The first being, "Now listen Bill, you don't eat just anyone's Gumbo because you don't know what they may have put in it". The second bit of advice, "You don't want to go to my Uncles' hunting camp if you are invited, they have never had a Yankee at their hunting camp and you don't know what they might have in mind". The first afternoon in rural Louisiana was just exactly how I pictured it. It was predictably hot and humid, and you could hear the deafening noise of the bugs in the middle of the day. My Uncles were all lined up on the porch to meet not only the Yankee that I married but the first one in the family. What a novelty he must have been to them! The first words spoken to Bill were from my Uncle Reese (better known as Cooter) as he was the head of the family after all. He says, "Hey Bill, some of the boys and I are going to the hunting camp this weekend and we're going to make a big ole pot of Gumbo. You wanna come"? That was the first and last time I have ever seen Bill speechless!

The Roux

There is just so much to say about Gumbo, and one who didn't know the dish well wouldn't know where to even begin! However, I do know that the heart of any Gumbo starts with a good roux. Patience and understanding the complexities of this french thickening base is the key. Not only does it thicken the Gumbo but this is where it gets its full bodied flavor from. As you follow the recipe just remember it takes time and constant babysitting and just when you think it will never work, it magically already has. You will watch it go from a blond to a brown color and finally to a dark chocolate brown. Watch it closely and when you have achieved the dark rich color and it smells like toasted nuts you have truly accomplished something wonderful! It is so easy to burn a roux so once it's the desired color, stop and remove it from the heat!

Step One: Preparing The Roux

1 cup vegetable oil
1 cup all purpose flour

Over medium heat add the oil to a 12 inch skillet and heat until it is hot. Slowly whisk in the flour, one spoonful at a time. Cook while whisking constantly. Minute by minute the flour will start to change color and the roux will begin to thicken. Just before the roux reaches a dark chocolate color take the pan off the heat immediately as it will continue to cook. Continue to whisk until it cools. Be patient as it can take up to 1 hour to cook to the desired color. You can use the Roux immediately or after it cools completely you can keep it in the refrigerator for a week or so.

Note: Before using the Roux that has been refrigerated bring it to room temperature before adding it to the Gumbo.

Yield: Makes 1 1/2 cups

Step Two: The Rice

2 cups long grain white rice, rinsed
4 cups water
2 teaspoons salt

In a medium size sauce pan add rice, water and salt. Bring to a gentle boil over medium high heat stirring occasionally. As soon as it starts boiling, lower heat to lowest setting and cover with a tight fitting lid. DO NOT OPEN LID until it has cooked for at least 20 minutes. Let rest and when ready to serve fluff with a fork.

Step Three: Preparing The Gumbo

1/4 cup vegetable oil
2 pounds chicken thighs, boneless, skinless, cut into 2 inch pieces
1 pound Chorizo, Andouille or Kielbasa sausage sliced into bite size pieces
6 cups chicken stock, divided
1 large onion, chopped
2 stalks celery, chopped
1 large green pepper, chopped
1/2 jalapeño pepper, seeded and minced
2 teaspoons salt
3 teaspoons pepper
2 tablespoons garlic, minced
Roux (see above recipe)
2 small bay leaves
2 teaspoons thyme
Tabasco sauce
1/2 cup fresh parsley, chopped (for garnish)
1/2 bunch green onions, chopped (for garnish)

Heat the oil in a large stock pot over medium high heat until hot. Add the chicken in batches and turn as they brown. As the chicken is done place in a shallow bowl to reserve the juices and set aside. Add the sausage and cook until lightly brown and fat is rendered out. Remove sausage and place in a separate bowl and set aside. Pour off all but 1/4 cup of fat from stock pot. Add 1/4 cup of chicken stock, scraping bottom to loosen any renderings remaining in the pot. Add onions, celery, green pepper and jalapeño, seasoning them with salt and pepper. Cook vegetables until soft over medium high heat. Add garlic and cook 1 minute more. Slowly add the roux and stir. Stir in the remaining chicken stock. Add the chicken thighs and juices. Add the bay leaves. Cover the pot and bring to a boil for one minute. Turn heat to the lowest simmer possible and cook for 2 hours while covered. Occasionally skim off the fat that floats to the top. Once the Gumbo gets a velvety texture add the sausage and season with thyme and a few drops of Tabasco sauce. Cook again at a low simmer for about 1/2 hour. Remove the bay leaves. Ladle Gumbo over 1/4 cup of white rice in a large bowls and garnish with parsley and green onions.

Note: I often serve this Gumbo with shrimp as well. During the last 20 minutes of cooking I drop about 1 pound of shrimp (pre-cooked, peeled, deveined and tails removed) into the Gumbo. The shrimp only needs enough time to heat through. You don't want to put them in too soon as they will over cook and get tough very quickly. You can also try many different variations of ingredients as you wish. A true Gumbo can have other types of seafood in it like crawfish, scallops, oysters, mussels or clams. You can be as creative as you wish!

Also, there is nothing better than a loaf of French Baguette bread, sliced on the bias, buttered and toasted under the broiler to serve along with the Gumbo.

Serves 6 to 8

Main Dishes

This is a wonderful recipe for Crab Cakes. I suggest serving it with either the Sweet Red Pepper Sauce or Elliot's Tartar Sauce recipe that you can find in this cookbook under "Sauces and Seasonings".

Caribbean Crab Cakes

1 pound fresh lump crab meat
2 teaspoons fresh marjoram, minced
2 eggs, beaten
1/2 cup mayonnaise
2 tablespoons whole grain mustard
1/2 cup green onions, chopped
1 tablespoon lemon zest
2 tablespoons lemon juice
1/2 cup clarified butter, divided
1 medium red bell pepper, finely diced
3/4 cup bread crumbs, unseasoned
salt and pepper to taste
1 cup flour
2 tablespoons capers
1/4 cup fresh parsley, chopped
lemon wedges

Preheat oven to 250 degrees.

Place the crab meat into a large bowl and gently flake apart with two forks. Add marjoram, eggs, mayonnaise, mustard, green onions, lemon zest and lemon juice. Combine well and set aside.

In a sauté pan over medium high heat add 2 tablespoons of the clarified butter. Once the butter is hot add the diced peppers. Sauté the peppers for 5 minutes or until tender. Remove the peppers from the pan with a slotted spoon and set aside to cool. Add the completely cooled peppers to the crab meat mixture along with the breadcrumbs, season with salt and pepper; mix to combine.

Form into 1 inch thick patties and dredge both sides in the flour, shaking off any excess. Heat a large nonstick skillet over medium high heat and add 3 or 4 tablespoons of clarified butter. Reserve any remaining clarified butter if you are cooking in batches. When the butter is hot add the crab cakes and cook about 5 minutes on each side until golden brown and crisp. If you are cooking in batches place the crab cakes on an ovenproof platter and keep warm in the oven until all of the patties are cooked. Before serving garnish with capers, parsley and lemon wedges.

Yield: Serves 6

Chicken Cordon Bleu

6 chicken breast, boneless and skinless
salt and pepper
1 pound ham, sliced thin
1 pound Swiss cheese, sliced thin
5 ounces fresh spinach, washed and stems removed
1 yard cooking twine
1 cup flour
6 eggs, beaten
1/2 teaspoon salt
1 tablespoon olive oil
3/4 cup bread crumbs, seasoned
3/4 cup Panko bread crumbs
1 1/2 cups Parmesan cheese, freshly grated
1 teaspoon garlic powder
1 teaspoon onion powder
1/2 teaspoon grated nutmeg
1 teaspoon thyme
1 teaspoon paprika
3/4 cup clarified butter (8 tablespoons for sautéing and 4 for serving)
2 tablespoons capers
1 lemon, cut into wedges
2 tablespoons parsley, minced

Preheat oven to 350 degrees.

Place one chicken breast at a time into a large resealable plastic bag and pound to flatten with the smooth end of a meat mallet to about 1/2 inch thick. Lightly salt and pepper the chicken.

Place 3 slices of ham, 2 slices of Swiss cheese and a small handful of spinach leaves on each breast. Roll the breast jelly roll style; secure with cooking string on both ends.

Prepare three different 8" pie plates with the following ingredients: pie plate one-flour, pie plate two-beaten eggs, salt and olive oil, pie plate three-bread crumbs, Parmesan cheese, garlic powder, onion powder, nutmeg, thyme and paprika.

Dredge the chicken in the flour mixture to coat well and shake off excess. Dip next in the egg and olive oil mixture then roll in the Parmesan and bread crumb mixture.

Heat 4 of the 8 tablespoons of butter in a large skillet over medium to medium high heat. Reserving the other 4 tablespoons of butter as you may need to cook the chicken in two batches. When the butter is hot add the chicken and sauté until golden brown on all sides being careful not to turn any more than necessary. Remove the chicken from the skillet and place on a baking sheet lined with parchment paper. Bake in the oven for 25 minutes or until the chicken is cooked through and the juices run clear.

Heat remaining 4 tablespoons of butter and pour over cooked chicken. Garnish with capers, lemon wedges and parsley.

Yield: Serves 6

Chicken Milanaise

4 chicken breast, boneless and skinless
salt and pepper, to taste
1 cup flour
6 eggs
1/2 teaspoon salt
1 tablespoon olive oil
1 1/2 cups Parmesan cheese, freshly grated
1 1/2 cups bread crumbs, seasoned
1 cup clarified butter
1 large bunch arugula
1/4 cup fresh parsley, chopped
1/4 cup capers
lemon wedges for garnish

Preheat oven to 200 degrees.

Place one chicken breast at a time into a large plastic bag and pound evenly with the smooth end of a mallet until it is 1/2 inch thick. Cut and trim into cutlets about the size of your palm. Season the cutlets with salt and pepper.

In an 8" pie plate, add flour. In another 8" pie plate, combine the eggs, salt and olive oil; beat well. In the third 8" pie plate, combine the Parmesan cheese and bread crumbs; mix well. One at a time, roll the cutlets in the flour and shake off excess. Dip the cutlets in the egg mixture and finish by rolling them gently in the cheese and bread crumb mixture; laying the cutlets on a baking sheet lined with wax paper as you continue (cutlets can be prepared ahead of time and refrigerated at this point if needed).

In a large saucepan add four to six tablespoons of the clarified butter and heat over medium to medium high heat until hot. Sauté the chicken on both sides until they are golden brown, about 3 to 5 minutes on each side. Do not force if they are stuck to the pan, you must wait until they release themselves and avoid turning more than once. Place on a warm ovenproof platter and keep in oven until all batches are done. Add clarified butter liberally to saucepan as needed while cooking each batch. Finish by laying each chicken cutlet on a bed of arugula; garnish with parsley, capers and lemon wedges. I like to serve with a drizzle of hot melted butter on top of each cutlet.

Yield: Serves 6 to 8

DRINK
Coca-Cola
ICE
COLD

Coca Cola Ham

1 spiral-sliced bone in ham, about 7 to 10 pounds
1 1/2 cups Coca Cola
2 cups honey or maple syrup
1/4 cup whole grain mustard
1/2 cup dark brown sugar
1/4 teaspoon nutmeg
1/2 teaspoon cinnamon
juice of 1/2 lemon

Preheat oven to 450 degrees.

Place the ham in a large roasting pan. Pour 1/2 cup of the Coca Cola over the ham. Bring the ham and Coca Cola to room temperature by letting it stand for 1 1/2 hours.

In a medium saucepan combine the remaining Coca Cola, honey, mustard, brown sugar, nutmeg, cinnamon and lemon juice. Bring to a gentle boil over medium heat while stirring often. Reduce the heat to low and simmer until it becomes thicker and a bit syrupy.

Brush some of the glaze over the ham. Place the ham in the oven for 20 minutes at 450 degrees. Remove the ham from the oven and brush it again with the glaze. Loosely tent with aluminum foil. Reduce the oven temperature to 250 degrees and bake for 3 1/2 hours. Baste the ham every 30 minutes with the glaze.

Remove the ham from the oven and let it rest for 20 minutes before carving. Combine the accumulated pan juices and any glaze left over; cook over medium heat until it has thickened. Serve the sauce with the ham.

Yield: Serves 16 to 20

This recipe is one of Bill's creations. It is the best corned beef and cabbage I have ever had! This is the corned beef just as it goes into the oven.

Corned Beef and Cabbage

Corned Beef:
10 pounds corned beef in brine
24 ounces stout
24 ounces lager
1/4 cup brown sugar
flavor packets from corned beef
10 cloves garlic, lightly mashed
20 whole peppercorns
8 sprigs fresh thyme
4 bay leaves
2 cups beef stock
water to cover plus two inches
10 yellow onions, cut into wedges
8 tablespoons butter

Vegetables:
1/4 cup vegetable oil
2 heads of cabbage, cut into 16 wedges
10 carrots, cut into 1 inch pieces
2 pounds red potatoes, cut into fourths
4 cups reserved braising liquid
4 tablespoons parsley, minced

Preheat oven to 300 degrees.

Corned Beef:
Rinse the corned beef thoroughly to remove excess salt and brine, place in roasting pan. Add the stout, lager and brown sugar. Add the flavor packets, garlic, peppercorns, thyme, bay leaves, stock, enough water to cover the meat plus two inches, onion wedges and butter. Bring to a gentle simmer over medium high heat and cook for 5 minutes. Cover and carefully place in the oven; cook 4 to 5 hours turning the meat halfway through. Remove the beef from the oven once it is fork tender and set aside. Reserve four cups of the braising liquid to cook with the cabbage.

Vegetables:
In a wide but large pot heat the oil on medium high. Once the oil is hot add the cabbage and cook until lightly browned on all sides about 6 to 8 minutes. Add the carrots and potatoes. Pour in the reserved braising liquid and bring to a simmer and cover. Turn the heat to low and cook for 10 to 15 minutes or until the cabbage is tender and slightly wilted. Remove the cabbage and set aside. Continue cooking the carrots and potatoes another 10 to 15 minutes or until tender.

Slice the corned beef against the grain and place it on a platter with the vegetables. Pour a bit of the braising liquid over the corned beef. Garnish with the parsley. Serve while hot.

Yield: Serves 12 to 18

French Hamburgers

8 tablespoons butter, room temperature and divided
1/2 cup onions, finely minced
1 1/2 pounds ground sirloin 85/15
salt and freshly ground pepper
1/4 cup fresh parsley, minced and divided
1 tablespoon fresh thyme, minced
1 egg, beaten
1/2 cup flour
1 tablespoon olive oil
1/2 cup beef stock

Preheat oven to 200 degrees.

Melt 2 tablespoons of the butter in a large skillet over medium high heat until hot. When the foam subsides add the onions and cook until translucent, about 5 minutes. Place the onions in a large mixing bowl and set aside to cool. Add the beef, salt, pepper, 2 tablespoons of the butter, 1 tablespoon of the parsley, thyme and egg to the onions; mix well. Form into patties about 3/4 inch thick. Add the flour to an eight inch pie plate and coat the patties with the flour; lightly shake off excess.

Place the oil and 2 tablespoons of the butter in the skillet and heat over medium high heat. When the butter and oil are hot add the patties and cook for about 3 to 5 minutes on each side for rare or more according to your preference. Place the patties in the oven to keep warm while you make the sauce.

Pour any extra fat out of the skillet. Add the beef stock and boil it down rapidly while scraping any renderings left in the pan from the patties. Continue to cook until stock becomes thicker and a bit syrupy. Remove from heat and add the remaining 2 tablespoons of butter and stir. Serve over hamburgers and garnish with parsley.

Yield: Serves 6

This is my absolute favorite place to be in the whole wide world! I adore this kitchen and especially this row of windows with the collection of antique honey tins, jars and pitchers. This is also one of my very favorite dishes. Its like eating candy! The fragrance of the rosemary from the garden is heaven "scent" in my book and it just makes me happy every time I have it on my cutting block. Lucky me!

Lamb Chops with Rosemary and Honey

24 lean loin lamb chops (about 3 ounces each and 1 inch thick)
salt and freshly ground pepper
2 tablespoons garlic, minced
1 jar (12 ounces) honey
1 jar (9 ounces) whole grain Dijon mustard
6 ounces fresh rosemary, leaves removed from stems and finely chopped (reserve a few sprigs for garnish)
1 lemon, sliced
1 jar (12 ounces) mint jelly

Place the lamb chops into a large shallow dish. Sprinkle with salt and pepper. Rub the minced garlic into the lamb.

Mix the honey and mustard together in a small bowl. Pour the honey and mustard mixture over the lamb and sprinkle generously with the rosemary. Cover with plastic wrap and place in the refrigerator for at least 6 hours to marinade or preferably overnight. Turn and rotate the lamb at least once while marinating.

Preheat outdoor grill to medium high heat.

Cook for 3 to 4 minutes on each side for rare, 4 to 5 on each side for medium and 5 to 6 for well done. While grilling continue to glaze the lamb with the marinade. Place the lamb on a serving platter and garnish with rosemary and lemon slices. Serve with mint jelly on the side.

Note: This recipe is best cooked on an outdoor grill. The honey causes quite a bit of smoking to occur.

Yield: Serves 6

Lamb Kabobs

1 cup balsamic vinegar
1/3 cup olive oil
zest of 4 lemons
1/4 cup fresh thyme, finely chopped
1/4 cup fresh oregano, finely chopped
1/4 cup fresh rosemary, finely chopped
1/2 cup garlic, minced
2 teaspoons salt
2 teaspoons pepper
2 pounds lamb tenderloin, cut into 1 1/2 inch pieces
2 large red bell peppers, seeded and cut into 1 1/2 inch pieces
2 medium red onions, halved crosswise and cut into wedges
1 package Pita bread
Cucumber and Dill Tzatziki Sauce (see recipe in section "Sauces and Seasonings")

In a shallow dish whisk together the vinegar, olive oil, lemon zest, thyme, oregano, rosemary, garlic, salt and pepper. Add the meat, red bell peppers and onions to the vinegar mixture; toss gently to coat. Let marinade overnight.

Preheat outdoor grill to medium high.

Thread the lamb onto metal skewers alternating between onions and red bell peppers. Place the kabobs on the grill and cook for 8 to 12 minutes turning often. Cook to desired temperature.

Warm the Pita bread on the grill. Serve the lamb kabobs wrapped in the Pita bread. Serve with the Cucumber and Dill Tzatziki Sauce.

Yield: Serves 6

Lemon and Rosemary Roasted Chicken

Chicken:
2 lemons
6 sprigs fresh rosemary, divided
4 cloves garlic, minced
3/4 cup butter, softened
1 whole chicken, rinsed and patted dry
salt and pepper to taste

Sauce:
1 tablespoon flour
1/2 cup dry white wine
1/2 cup chicken stock

Preheat oven to 350 degrees.

Zest the two lemons into a medium size bowl. Strip the leaves from two sprigs of rosemary and finely chop. Place the rosemary, garlic and butter in the bowl with the lemon zest. Salt and pepper to taste; combine well.

Using your hands massage the butter mixture all over the dry chicken, under the skin and inside the cavity as well. Cut one of the lemons in half and squeeze the juice over the chicken. Cut the second lemon into slices and place inside the cavity of the chicken along with two rosemary sprigs.

Place the chicken in a roasting pan with a raised rack. Roast in oven for 20 minutes per pound. Lightly tent with foil the first half of cooking so the skin doesn't over brown. Remove the foil during the last half of cooking. When the chicken is done the skin should be deep golden brown and juices should be running clear. You should be able to cut between a leg and a thigh easily. A meat thermometer inserted into the inner thigh should read 165 degrees.

Remove the chicken from the oven when it is completely cooked through and place on a platter. Lightly tent with foil and let rest while you make the sauce.

Drain off the fat while leaving about two tablespoons of accumulated juices from the roasting pan. Place the roasting pan over medium high heat. Add the flour; stir to combine with pan juices and brown bits. Add the wine and whisk briskly while cooking for a few minutes. Add the chicken stock and stir until reduced by 1/4. The sauce should thicken slightly. Check for seasonings and turn the heat to low. Carve the chicken, serve with the sauce and garnish with the remaining rosemary sprigs.

Yield: Serves 4 to 6

"The Keeper of the Gate"

Lime and Garlic Pork Tenderloin

2 pounds pork tenderloin
juice of 1 lime
2 tablespoons garlic, minced
salt and freshly ground pepper
1 cup all purpose flour
1/4 cup clarified butter
1 1/2 cups chicken stock
1 small bay leaf
2 tablespoons heavy cream
1/2 cup fresh parsley, finely chopped

Place the tenderloins in a shallow dish. Sprinkle with the lime juice, minced garlic, salt and pepper. Cover with plastic wrap and marinade for at least 4 hours or preferably overnight.

Just before cooking place the flour in a shallow dish long enough to accommodate the tenderloins. Roll the tenderloins in the flour to coat evenly and shake off excess.

Add the clarified butter to a large skillet and heat over medium high heat until hot. Once the butter is hot add the tenderloins while gently turning to brown on all sides. Do not force the tenderloins if they are stuck to the bottom of the pan. You will need to wait for them to release themselves. Avoid turning too often.

Once the tenderloins are browned on all sides turn heat to medium low and slowly add chicken stock until it is up to about 1/4 of the sides of the tenderloins. Add the bay leaf and bring to a gentle boil. Once boiling immediately turn the heat to a low simmer, cover and cook for 45 minutes or until fork tender.

Remove the tenderloins to a warm platter. Let rest for 15 minutes and slice into 1/2 inch medallions. Discard the bay leaf. Add the heavy cream to the sauce and reduce until slightly thickened. Pour the sauce over the meat and garnish with the parsley.

Yield: Serves 6 to 8

Meatloaf

1/2 cup butter
1 cup green bell pepper, finely chopped
1 cup onion, finely chopped
2 teaspoons garlic, minced
1 pound ground sirloin, lean
1 pound ground veal
1 pound ground turkey
1 pound sweet Italian sausage
2 packages Lipton Onion Soup Mix
1/2 cup parsley, finely chopped
2 eggs, room temperature and beaten
1/2 cup Worcestershire sauce
1 teaspoon salt
1 teaspoon pepper
1 cup ketchup

Preheat oven to 350 degrees.

In a medium skillet over medium high heat melt the butter. When the foam subsides add the peppers, onions and garlic, sauté until soft. Set aside and let cool.

In an extra large bowl add all of the ingredients together except for the ketchup. I suggest wearing food safe plastic gloves and mixing by hand until all of the ingredients are well incorporated.

Place the meat into two separate loaf pans. Bake for 1 1/2 hours. About every 30 minutes pour off the fat that has accumulated into a heat proof disposable container. During the last 15 minutes of cooking spread the ketchup over the loaves and continue to cook.

Pour off any remaining fat and transfer to a serving platter. Let the meatloaf rest for 15 minutes. Cut into 1/2 inch thick slices and serve.

Note: You can always freeze one loaf uncooked for a future meal. After freezing and when ready to use thaw the meatloaf completely, bring to room temperature and cook as directed.

Yield: Serves 12

Fresh 'SALADA' TEA Delicious

Papa's Prime Rib

prime rib roast of beef, about six ribs
1/2 cup apple cider vinegar

generous amounts of:
coarse sea salt
freshly ground pepper
Italian seasoning
garlic powder
onion powder

Preheat oven to 500 degrees on BROIL.

Place prime rib (bone side down) in a 2 inch deep roasting pan. Pour the apple cider vinegar over the meat. Sprinkle the salt and pepper generously over the entire roast making a thick layer. Sprinkle the Italian seasoning, garlic powder and onion powder generously on the roast and massage in with your hands covering all sides. Insert a meat thermometer into center of roast, careful not to touch a bone. Broil in oven for about 15 minutes or until the roast is seared.

Reduce oven to 250 degrees on BAKE.

Bake until desired temperature is reached. Remove from oven and let rest for 30 minutes before carving.

Rare-15 minutes per pound or 140 degrees internally
Medium Rare-20 minutes per pound or 155 degrees internally
Medium-25 minutes per pound or 160 degrees internally
Well-30 minutes per pound or 170 degrees internally

I recommend taking the roast out about 10 degrees before it reaches the desired temperature because the meat will continue to cook while resting. Let rest for about 20 minutes before carving.

MAMA'S PRIME RIB
Follow the recipe above omitting the apple cider vinegar and rubbing the roast thoroughly with olive oil and adding generous amounts of the above salt, pepper and spices by massaging it in with your hands on all sides. Place in roasting pan on a roasting rack and cook according to directions above.

Yield: Serves 6

GONE FISHIN'

Tilapia with Chipotle Peppers in Adobo Sauce

2 tilapia fillets (8 ounces each)
1/4 teaspoon salt
1/4 teaspoon pepper
3 tablespoons olive oil
1/4 cup shallots, finely chopped
1/2 tablespoon garlic, minced
1/2 cup dry white wine
1/2 cup chicken stock
2 tablespoons heavy cream
3 tablespoons cold butter
1 tablespoon cilantro, chopped
1 1/2 tablespoons chipotle peppers in Adobo sauce, finely chopped

Preheat oven to 250 degrees.

Season the tilapia fillets with salt and pepper on both sides. In a large non-stick skillet heat the olive oil over medium high heat. When the oil is hot add the tilapia and sauté on first side for about 3 minutes. Once the fillets start looking opaque on the edges and they release from the pan easily gently flip onto other side. Cook for 3 minutes on second side. Only flip fillets once as they need to be handled carefully. If the fillets are slightly undercooked at this point they will continue to cook in the oven while you are preparing the sauce. Remove the fish from the skillet and place on an oven proof platter in the preheated oven to keep warm until the sauce is prepared.

In the same skillet over medium high heat add the shallots and garlic. Cook for 3 minutes or just until slightly translucent. Add the white wine and bring to a gentle simmer and cook until reduced by half while stirring to scrape up any crusty brown bits. Add the chicken stock and bring to a gentle boil and reduce the heat to low. Simmer, uncovered for about 10 minutes or until liquid is reduced to about 1/4 cup.

Stir in the heavy cream. Add the butter one tablespoon at a time, stirring until the butter is melted after each addition. Sauce should be slightly thickened. Add the cilantro and the chipotle peppers in Adobo sauce. Stir to combine and serve the sauce over the fish. Serve immediately.

Yield: Serves 2

There is nothing like taking a little quiet time for yourself out on the water.

Veal Piccata

2 pounds veal cutlets
salt and freshly ground pepper
1/4 cup all purpose flour
1 tablespoon olive oil
1/4 cup butter, divided
1 cup dry white wine
1 cup chicken stock
2 lemons, divided
1 tablespoon garlic, minced
2 tablespoons fresh parsley, chopped
2 tablespoons capers

Preheat oven to 200 degrees.

Place each cutlet between wax paper and with the smooth end of a meat mallet pound the veal until it is about 1/4 inch thick. Cut veal into pieces about the size of your palm. Salt and pepper the veal. Add the flour to a shallow dish and lightly coat the veal on both sides, shaking off excess.

Add the oil and 2 tablespoons of the butter to a large skillet and heat on medium high. Once the oil and butter are hot add the veal and cook 3 minutes on each side or until lightly browned. Do not over crowd the pan with the meat otherwise it will steam and not brown (you may need to cook in batches). Also do not overcook the veal as it will become tough. Remove the veal from the skillet and transfer to an oven proof platter and place in the oven to keep warm.

Add remaining butter to the skillet and heat through while scraping pan to loosen any renderings. Once butter is hot and the foam has subsided add the wine, chicken stock, juice of one lemon and the garlic. Continue to cook over medium high heat while stirring constantly and reduce the sauce by half. Pour the sauce over the veal.

Garnish with lemon slices, fresh parsley and capers.

Serve immediately.

Yield: Serves 4

Veal with Basil, Prosciutto and Mozzarella

6 veal cutlets, about 1 1/2 pounds
salt and fresh ground pepper
1/2 pound Prosciutto Di Parma, 18 paper thin slices
1 pound mozzarella cheese, sliced
18 basil leaves
cooking twine
1/4 cup olive oil
1/2 cup shallots, chopped
2 tablespoons garlic, minced
1 cup dry white wine
1 cup chicken stock
1/2 cup diced tomatoes
1/2 cup tomato puree
2 teaspoons fresh oregano, chopped
2 teaspoons fresh thyme, chopped
1/4 cup fresh parsley, chopped
1/2 cup sliced cherry tomatoes
crushed red pepper to taste
1/2 cup Parmesan cheese, shredded

Preheat oven to 200 degrees.

Place a veal cutlet between two pieces of wax paper and pound lightly with a flat mallet until it is about 1/4 inch thick. Continue until all cutlets are pounded. Dry veal throughly with paper towels.

Sprinkle with salt and pepper. Place three slices of Prosciutto and two slices of mozzarella cheese on top of each cutlet following with three basil leaves. Roll up the veal cutlets cigar style starting at the bottom and rolling toward the top. Tie with cooking twine on each end to hold it together.

Heat the oil on medium high heat in a saucepan large enough to hold all of the veal in one layer without crowding. When hot, add the veal and sauté on all sides for a few minutes until you have achieved a light brown color. Do not overcook. Remove the veal from the pan and place on an oven proof platter. Place the veal in the oven to keep warm while you make the sauce. Add the shallots to the pan and cook while stirring for about 3 minutes. Add the garlic and cook for an additional 3 minutes. Add the wine and let it simmer with the shallots and garlic for a few minutes to reduce slightly. Add the stock and cook to reduce by half. Add the diced tomatoes, tomato puree, oregano and thyme to the pan and mix well. Bring to a very gentle boil. Add the veal back to the pan. Turn heat to lowest setting, cover and simmer for 25 minutes. Remove cooking twine and serve veal and sauce over your choice of pasta. Garnish with fresh parsley, cherry tomatoes, crushed red pepper and Parmesan cheese. Serve immediately.

Yield: Serves 6

Aunt Genevieve's Halupki

I remember so well the rainy and cold winter day that my dear friend Kathy invited me over to her Aunt Genevieve's home to learn the art of making Halupki. I was a recent resident of upstate New York and was mesmerized by the difference in the northern food from the southern food that I was raised on. Halupki being one of them, not only had I never heard of it but I couldn't even pronounce it! Aunt Genevieve was so gracious as she taught us to make this wonderful dish in her tiny, clean and very organized kitchen. I was also pregnant at the time and very hungry!

1 small head of cabbage, cleaned, cored and leaves separated
1 pound ground beef
1/4 pound ground pork
1 1/2 cups cooked white rice
2 eggs, beaten
1 tablespoon garlic, minced
1 medium onion, finely chopped
salt and freshly ground pepper
1 bunch fresh parsley, chopped and divided
2 cans condensed tomato soup (no water added)
1 1/2 cups chicken stock
1 bay leaf

Place the cabbage leaves in a large pot of salted boiling water. Water should come halfway up to the cabbage. Turn cabbage halfway through cooking. Cook cabbage leaves only until they are soft and pliable. Take leaves out as they cook and dip in an ice water bath to stop the cooking process. Set aside and drain on paper towels.

In a large mixing bowl add the meat, rice, egg, garlic, onion, salt, pepper and 1/4 of the parsley; mix well. Remove and discard the thick stems of the cabbage leaves. Fill the center of each leaf with about three tablespoons of the meat mixture and roll tightly. Pour 1/2 can of tomato soup and chicken stock into the bottom of a large stock pot along with some of the parsley and 1/2 of the bay leaf. Layer the rolled cabbage, tomato soup, parsley and the remaining portion of the bay leaf ending with tomato soup on top. Simmer on low heat for 1 1/2 hours while partially covered with a lid.

Yield: Serves 8

Bubble and Squeak

I only remember one cookbook in our home as a child. We had the ever trusty Fannie Farmer and it was like a bible to us three girls as we honed our skills in the kitchen. This recipe is one that Mom cooked often from this reliable cookbook and it brings back many memories. I took a few liberties of my own with this British dish but I think the few enhancements are all the better for it. What I wouldn't give to have that original cookbook back. I would love to see all of the mark ups, chicken scratch and hand written notes created by our teenage hands.

1 medium head of cabbage, cored and cut into medium size pieces
1 1/2 cups chicken stock
1 pound sausage meat, ground
1/2 medium onion, chopped
4 tablespoons butter
4 tablespoons flour
1 teaspoon salt
1/2 teaspoon pepper
2 cups whole milk
pinch nutmeg, grated
1/2 cup bread crumbs

Preheat oven to 350 degrees.

Prepare a 2 quart casserole dish with cooking spray and set aside.

Add the chopped cabbage to a medium size skillet with the chicken stock and sauté over medium high heat just until soft. Drain and set aside.

Cook the sausage in a skillet, breaking it up into small pieces as it browns. Cook thoroughly and remove the meat from the skillet; set aside. Add the chopped onion to the skillet and cook until soft and translucent; set aside. Add the meat and onions to the bottom of the prepared casserole dish. Cover the meat and onions with the cooked cabbage; set aside.

In a medium skillet melt the butter over medium low heat and slowly add the flour, salt and pepper. Using a whisk stir until it is a smooth paste. Continue to cook for about 2 to 3 minutes but do not let it brown. Reduce the heat to low and slowly add the milk, stirring constantly until thick and smooth. Watch carefully as it will scald on the bottom. Add the nutmeg and stir. Cover the sausage, onions and cabbage with the white sauce.

Sprinkle the bread crumbs over the top of the casserole.

Bake for 30 to 40 minutes or until bubbling hot.

Yield: Serves 6

Cajun Shrimp

2 bottles beer (any brand)
1/2 cup apple cider vinegar
2 cups water
2 tablespoons Old Bay Seasoning
2 pounds large shrimp (31/35), uncooked, peeled and deveined
2 tablespoons fresh garlic, minced
1 1/2 tablespoons Cajun Seasoning (see recipe in section "Sauces and Seasonings")
juice of 1 lemon
1/4 cup fresh parsley, finely chopped

Pour the beer, vinegar and water into a stock pot. Add the Old Bay Seasoning and bring to a boil. Once the liquid is boiling add the shrimp. Cover and cook for 2 minutes or until the shrimp turn pink and the flesh is opaque. Do not overcook. Drain the shrimp in a colander and layer with ice to chill and stop the cooking process.

Place the shrimp into a large bowl and toss with the garlic, Cajun Seasoning and lemon juice. Garnish with fresh parsley. This dish can be served warm or cold.

Yield: Serves 8

Chicken Pot Pie

This recipe is a family favorite and comfort food at its best. My father in-law, Floyd really enjoyed this dish. Whenever he joined us for Sunday dinner he was always delighted to hear "Chicken Pot Pie" was on the menu! I loved cooking for him as he was always one of my biggest fans when it came to my culinary activities! Keep in mind that this dish can easily be transformed into Chicken and Biscuits by omitting the pie crust and the eggs and serving over hot biscuits.

4 tablespoons butter
2 generous tablespoons flour
1/2 teaspoon salt
1/4 teaspoon fresh ground pepper
2 cups chicken stock
2 tablespoons half and half
1 1/2 pounds cooked chicken (white or dark meat), cut into bite size pieces
2 hard boiled eggs, peeled and sliced
1 package prepared pie crust (2 crust), room temperature

Preheat oven to 425 degrees.

Melt the butter in a large skillet over medium high heat and slowly add the flour; stir to form a smooth paste. Add salt and pepper. Continue to cook for 3 minutes or until the flour has a light golden color. Slowly add chicken stock, stirring to keep mixture smooth. Add the half and half. Reduce heat to medium low and cook stirring constantly for about 10 minutes or until sauce thickens (the sauce should cling to a spoon). Remove from heat, add chicken and sliced boiled eggs; stir gently to combine.

Remove one pie crust from the package and place it in the bottom of a pie plate. Pour chicken mixture into the pie crust. Remove second pie shell from package and place it on top of chicken mixture. Tuck the pie shell under on the edges and flute with a fork or your fingers. Pierce pie crust in center by making two slits for steam to escape. Cover edges with a pie shield or make one with aluminum foil. Bake for 35 to 45 minutes or until bubbling and golden brown on top. Remove pie shield halfway through cooking.

Note: Do not continue to cook on stove once boiled eggs are added as they will become tough.

Yield: Serves 4 to 6

Lamb Sausage

2 pounds lamb shoulder
1/2 pound bacon
1/2 pound chicken thighs, boneless and skinless
1/4 cup garlic, coarsely chopped
2 tablespoons fresh marjoram, minced
2 tablespoons fresh thyme, minced
1/2 bunch fresh cilantro, finely chopped
1/4 cup fresh ginger, minced
salt and freshly ground pepper
medium pig casings (optional)
2 tablespoons vegetable oil

Cut the lamb, bacon and chicken into 1/2 inch cubes. In a large bowl combine the meat with the garlic, marjoram, thyme, cilantro and ginger.

Mix well, cover and let marinade overnight in the refrigerator.

The following day grind the mixture through a meat grinder with a 1/2 inch blade. Place back into the bowl and season with salt and pepper. Stir to combine.

Stuff into medium pig casings and tie into 5 inch links or form into patties.

Add the vegetable oil to a large skillet and heat over medium high heat. When the oil is hot add the sausage and fry while turning to cook on both sides until cooked thoroughly and browned.

Yield: Serves 12

Louisiana Red Beans and Rice

1 pound dry red kidney beans
1 pound bacon, cut into 1 inch pieces
1 small green pepper, chopped
2 celery stalks, chopped
1 medium onion, chopped
4 cloves garlic, chopped
1 pound Chorizo, Andouille or Kielbasa sausage, cut into 1 inch slices
2 tablespoons fresh parsley, chopped
1/8 teaspoon red pepper flakes
2 teaspoons cumin
1 teaspoon chili powder
1 large bay leaf
1 ham bone with generous amounts of meat
1 teaspoon dried basil
2 tablespoons Worcestershire sauce
1 can (15 ounces) tomato sauce
salt and pepper to taste
4 cups cooked rice

Wash and pick over the beans. Cover in fresh cold water and soak overnight.

In a large skillet fry the bacon and place on paper towels to drain. In the bacon drippings sauté the green pepper, celery, onion and garlic until soft and translucent. Remove the vegetables from the skillet and place in a bowl and set aside. Add the sausage to the same skillet and sear until brown and the fat is rendered out.

In a large stock pot add the beans and water in which they were soaked in. Add the cooked bacon, sautéed vegetables and sausage. Add all of the other ingredients and more water to cover if necessary. Bring to a gentle boil and immediately lower the heat to a simmer while partially covered. Simmer for about 1 1/2 hours or until the beans are tender. Adjust seasoning if necessary. Remove bay leaf and ham bone. Serve over warm white rice in bowls.

Yield: Serves 8 to 10

Penne Carbonara

This is a great recipe that is easy and quick, however you need to have all of the ingredients prepared and ready to go because everything comes together at once. You won't have time to stop and chop an onion!

16 ounces penne pasta
16 ounces pancetta
1/2 cup shallots, minced
1 cup half and half, room temperature
2 eggs, room temperature and beaten
salt and freshly ground pepper
1 cup Pecorino Romano cheese, freshly grated
1/4 cup fresh parsley, chopped

Prepare all of the above ingredients and have them at hand.

In a large pot cook the penne pasta in boiling salted water for about 11 minutes or according to package directions for al dente. Immediately remove from heat, rinse with cool water to stop the cooking process, drain and set aside. In a large skillet over medium high heat, add the pancetta and cook until just crisp. Add the shallots to the skillet with the pancetta and cook until translucent. While keeping the pancetta and shallots hot over medium heat, add the drained pasta and toss gently together. In a medium bowl pour the half and half into the beaten egg and mix together. Pour egg mixture over the pasta and toss gently again. Heat thoroughly and sprinkle with the cheese. Toss once more and garnish with the fresh parsley. Remove from heat and serve immediately.

Note: It is very important that the half and half and the egg are room temperature before preparing this dish. If they are cold when you add them to the skillet you will unfortunately have scrambled eggs instead of creamy pasta.

Yield: Serves 6 to 8

Penne Pasta with Chicken, Tomatoes and Spinach

1 pound penne pasta
4 chicken breast, boneless and skinless, cut into bite size pieces
salt and pepper to taste
4 tablespoons butter, divided
1 package (8 ounces) mushrooms, sliced
2 tablespoons olive oil
4 cloves garlic, minced
3/4 cup dry white wine
3/4 cup chicken stock
2 cups grape or cherry tomatoes, halved lengthwise
12 stalks cooked asparagus, al dente
6 ounces fresh spinach
4 ounces Parmesan cheese, shaved
8 basil leaves, coarsely chopped
crushed red pepper to taste

Cook pasta according to the package directions in salted water. Drain and rinse in cool water to stop the cooking process; set aside. Sprinkle chicken with salt and pepper; set aside.

Heat 2 tablespoons of the butter in a medium size skillet. When the skillet is hot add the mushrooms; sauté until golden brown. Remove mushrooms from the skillet and set aside.

Heat 2 tablespoons of the butter and the olive oil over medium high heat in a large skillet. Add the chicken in a single layer and brown on both sides. Sauté until completely cooked through, remove from the skillet and set aside.

Turn the heat to medium and add the garlic to the skillet; quickly stir to avoid burning. After 1 minute pour in the wine and stock, stirring to deglaze the pan. Allow the liquid to gently boil and continue cooking until it is reduced by half.

Turn off the heat. Add the tomatoes, mushrooms, asparagus, spinach, chicken and cooked pasta to the skillet. Toss to combine. Generously add Parmesan cheese.

Garnish with more Parmesan cheese, fresh cut basil and crushed red pepper to taste.

Yield: Serves 4 to 6

Pork Chops and Stuffing

Stuffing:
4 tablespoons butter
1 cup celery, finely chopped
1 cup onion, finely chopped
2 cups chicken stock
1 bag (12 ounces) cubed herb stuffing mix
1 teaspoon sage
1/2 teaspoon poultry seasoning
2 eggs, room temperature and beaten
salt and pepper to taste

Sauce:
4 tablespoons butter
2 tablespoons all purpose flour
2 cups chicken stock
2 tablespoons heavy cream
salt and pepper to taste

Pork Chops:
6 Pork Chops, bone in and 1 1/2 inches thick, patted dry
salt and pepper to taste
1/4 cup vegetable oil

Preheat oven to 325 degrees. Prepare a13x9x2 inch baking dish with cooking spray.

Stuffing: Prepare stuffing by adding butter to a medium size skillet over medium high heat. When the foam subsides add the celery and onions; cook for about 5 minutes or until vegetables are soft and transculent. Add the stock, stir to combine and remove from heat. Add stuffing, sage and poultry seasoning to the vegetables and broth. Let cool significantly and add eggs. Stir to combine well. Salt and pepper to taste; set aside.

Sauce: In a medium size skillet over medium heat add the butter. When the foam subsides, add the flour and stir constantly while making a paste. Continue to cook for 3 minutes or until paste is golden in color. Slowly add the chicken stock while stirring to keep the mixture smooth. Add the heavy cream. Add salt and pepper to taste. Cook stirring constantly until mixture thickens slightly, about 10 minutes. Remove from heat and set aside.

Pork Chops: Salt and pepper the pork chops. Heat vegetable oil in a large skillet. When the oil is hot place the pork chops in the skillet and brown on each side. Remove pork chops and place in prepared baking dish in a single layer.

With an ice cream scoop place a generous ball of stuffing on top of each pork chop. Pour all of the cooked sauce over the pork chops and stuffing.

Cover with foil and bake at 325 degrees for 1 hour. Remove foil and uncover for the last 15 minutes of cooking.

Yield: Serves 6

Pot Roast

1 cup all purpose flour
salt and freshly ground pepper
3 to 4 pounds boneless chuck roast
1/4 cup vegetable oil
2 stalks celery, chopped
2 medium carrots, chopped
1 medium onion, quartered
3 cloves garlic, minced
1/2 cup red wine
4 cups beef stock
1 package Lipton Onion Soup Mix
1 bay leaf
2 tablespoons tomato paste
2 tablespoons all purpose flour dissolved in 1/4 cup water
1 teaspoon thyme

Place flour, salt and pepper in a large baking dish. Place roast in the flour and coat well; shake off excess. Add the oil to a large Dutch oven over medium high heat. When the oil is hot add the roast and brown on both sides. Remove roast from Dutch oven and set aside. Add the vegetables and garlic to the pot and cook over medium high heat; stirring often until softened. Add the wine and cook while scraping the bottom of the pot until the wine has reduced by half. Add the beef stock, Lipton Onion Soup Mix, bay leaf and the tomato paste. Return the roast back to the pot and cover with a lid. Roast should be almost covered with stock during cooking. If additional stock is needed while roast is cooking add a little at a time. Cook for 3 to 4 hours at a very low simmer until fork tender. Remove the meat from the pot to an oven safe dish and keep warm in the oven on a very low temperature. Strain the vegetables and broth in a fine seive, reserving broth and discarding vegetables. Skim the fat off of the surface of the broth and discard. Add the broth back into the Dutch Oven. Stir in the flour and water mixture. Turn the heat up to medium high and cook the broth while scraping the bottom of the pan. Stirring constantly until the broth has reduced and thickened. Add the thyme and cook five more minutes. Salt and pepper to taste. Slice the meat and serve it with the thickened beef broth.

Yield: Serves 6 to 8

Salmon with Lemon and Dill

4 salmon fillets, 8 ounces each
salt and pepper
2 tablespoons fresh dill, finely chopped
4 tablespoons butter
2 lemons, thinly sliced
2 tablespoons capers
4 aluminum foil squares, 12"x12"

Preheat oven to 350 degrees.

Place a salmon fillet in the center of each square of aluminum foil. Sprinkle each piece of fish with salt, pepper, fresh dill, 1 tablespoon of butter, 2 to 3 lemon slices and 1 tablespoon of capers. Neatly fold the aluminum foil into tidy packets, sealing tightly. Place packages directly on a baking sheet and bake in the oven for 20 minutes. Let rest for 5 to 10 minutes before opening packets. Salmon should be opaque, tender and flaky when done. Use caution when you are opening the foil packets as they release hot steam.

Yield: Serves 4

Shrimp Creole

- 2 cups onions, chopped
- 1/2 cup green onions, chopped
- 1 cup green bell pepper, chopped
- 1 cup celery, chopped
- 2 cloves garlic, minced
- 1 teaspoon fresh thyme, minced
- 1/4 cup vegetable oil
- 4 tablespoons flour
- 3 teaspoons salt
- 1/2 teaspoon pepper
- 1 can (6 ounces) tomato paste
- 1 can (16 ounces) crushed tomatoes
- 1 can (16 ounces) tomato sauce
- 1 cup chicken stock
- 2 bay leaves
- 4 pounds large shrimp (31/35), uncooked, peeled and deveined
- 1 teaspoon Tabasco sauce
- 1/2 cup fresh parsley, chopped
- juice of 1 lemon
- 4 cups cooked white rice

Chop the onions, green onions, green bell pepper and celery. Mince the garlic and thyme; set aside.

In a 4 quart dutch oven make a dark brown roux by heating the oil over medium to medium high heat until hot. Slowly add the flour one tablespoon at a time while whisking constantly. Watch carefully as it can burn very easily. Once you have achieved a dark brown color the roux is finished. Add the chopped vegetables quickly so the roux doesn't over brown or burn. Add the garlic, thyme, salt and pepper; sauté uncovered over medium heat until the vegetables are translucent and soft, about 30 minutes.

Add the tomato paste and sauté for 3 minutes. Add the crushed tomatoes, tomato sauce, chicken stock and bay leaves. Simmer on low heat while partially covered for one hour, stirring occasionally.

Add the shrimp and cook until they are just done, about 5 minutes. The shrimp are cooked when they turn pink and opaque. Do not overcook the shrimp. Add the Tabasco sauce, parsley and lemon juice; stir to combine. Cover and remove from heat. Serve over rice.

This dish is best when it is allowed to marinade several hours or overnight in the refrigerator. Let cool completely before refrigerating.

To reheat; remove from the refrigerator and bring to room temperature one hour before reheating. Heat quickly without boiling so as not to overcook the shrimp and serve immediately.

Yield: Serves 8 to 10

Beef Stroganoff

2 1/2 pounds beef tenderloin, cut into 1 1/2 strips
salt and pepper to taste
1/4 cup olive oil
3 tablespoons butter
1 package (8 ounces) mushrooms, sliced
3 medium shallots, finely chopped (about 1/2 cup)
1 tablespoon garlic, minced
1 1/2 cups red wine
2 cups beef stock
1 tablespoon Dijon mustard
1 cup sour cream, room temperature
1 cup cream cheese, room temperature
1 teaspoon thyme
1 package (12 ounces) dry egg noodles
2 tablespoons parsley, chopped

In order to insure a nice sear on the meat pat it dry with paper towels to remove any excess moisture. Sprinkle with salt and pepper. In a large skillet over medium high heat add the olive oil and heat until hot. Add the beef to the skillet but do not overcrowd the meat as it will steam and not brown. If you need to cook the meat in a couple of smaller batches then do so. Quickly brown the beef stirring once or twice, cooking the beef to rare. Almost as soon as you put the beef in the pan it will be time to take it out. Do not overcook it as it will cook a bit more when you add it to the sauce. Remove the beef from the pan and place it in a large bowl reserving all of the pan juices and set aside.

In the same skillet add the butter and heat over medium high heat. Add the mushrooms and sauté while stirring often until golden brown. Remove the mushrooms and their juices from the skillet and place in the same bowl as the meat; set aside. Add the shallots to the skillet and sauté for 3 minutes. Add the garlic and sauté an additional minute. Add the red wine and simmer until it is reduced by half. Add the beef stock and simmer for another 10 to 15 minutes. All of the liquid should have reduced and should ever so slightly cling to a spoon. Add the Dijon mustard and stir to combine. Reduce heat to low; add the sour cream and cream cheese while whisking to incorporate. Bring to a gentle simmer and continue to cook until sauce has thickened slightly. Add the thyme, beef and mushrooms to the sauce. Heat just until all of the ingredients are heated completely through without over cooking the meat.

Meanwhile cook the egg noodles according to the package directions for al dente. Once the noodles are cooked drain them in a colander. Place the cooked noodles in a large shallow bowl. Pour sauce and meat over the noodles and toss to combine. Garnish with chopped parsley. Serve while hot.

Serves 6

Note: If you are doubling or tripling this recipe you may find that adding a slurry of 1 cup room temperature beef broth and 2 tablespoons of cornstarch will help thicken the sauce. Add the mixture in a little at a time until you have the consistency that you like.

Bill's Italian Tomato Sauce and Meatballs

If you were to say that Bill is passionate about his sauce and meatballs it would be an understatement to say the least! He puts his whole heart and soul into this recipe and then some. It's not your average dish that you just "whip" together, in fact it's quite a production. He usually requires a sous chef because it's so labor intensive. He also does not know how to make this dish for just a few people, only in batches to accommodate about 50 people. The following recipe makes about 120 meatballs and the sauce is cooked in a 32 quart stock pot. It's a lot of work, quite impressive and so very good! You can taste that passion in every bite. There are two things you can count on when you smell the heavenly scents coming from the kitchen. One being, it's going to be scrumptious and two just like clockwork Bill will say, "This just might be the best sauce and meatballs you have ever had".

Italian Tomato Sauce:
6 tablespoons olive oil
2 medium onions, minced
1/2 cup garlic, minced
1 1/2 bottles red wine
10 quarts tomatoes, combinations of tomato sauce, crushed tomatoes or fresh "Roasted Tomatoes" pureed (see note below)
1 quart plain applesauce
3 tablespoons fresh basil, minced
4 tablespoons fresh oregano, minced
2 tablespoons fresh parsley, minced
1 tablespoon dried Italian seasoning
1/2 tablespoon pepper
1 tablespoon salt
3 tablespoons sugar
1/2 teaspoon cayenne pepper
1 teaspoon crushed red pepper
1 teaspoon dried thyme

Heat the olive oil in a very large stock pot (32 quarts) until hot, add the onions and garlic; sauté until translucent. Add 1 cup of the wine and deglaze the pot. Add the remaining wine and all of the ingredients with the exception of the thyme; stir to combine. Bring to a gentle boil and immediately reduce the heat to a very low simmer. Add the meatballs (recipe follows). Simmer uncovered on very low heat for eight hours; stirring occasionally. Add the thyme an hour before serving. Serve over hot pasta.

Note: You can find the recipe for the fresh Roasted Tomatoes in the section "Sides Dishes" in this cookbook. They are a wonderful addition to the sauce in lieu of canned tomatoes. Puree the Roasted Tomatoes in a kitchen blender before adding to the sauce.

Serves about 50

Meatballs:
2 large onions, minced
2 pounds Italian sweet sausage
2 pounds Italian hot sausage
2 pounds ground chuck, 80/20
2 pounds ground sirloin, 85/15
4 eggs
5 tablespoons garlic, minced
15 ounces bread crumbs, seasoned
4 teaspoons pepper
4 teaspoons salt
4 teaspoons Italian seasoning
2 teaspoons dried oregano
2 teaspoons garlic salt
2 teaspoons cayenne pepper
4 ounces Parmesan cheese, shredded
2 tablespoons fresh parsley, chopped

Preheat oven to 350 degrees.

Lightly coat four large baking sheets with cooking spray and set aside.

In a very large bowl combine all of the ingredients and mix thoroughly with your hands. Pat and roll the mixture together and form into balls about the size of golf balls. Place the meatballs on the baking sheets in rows of 4. Do not over crowd as they will steam and not brown.

Place in the oven and bake for 30 minutes or until lightly browned and just cooked through.

Place the meatballs in the sauce. Continue to simmer on low heat until the sauce is finished.

Makes about 120 meatballs.

Chicken Enchiladas in Mole Sauce

Mole Sauce:
2 teaspoons chili powder
1/2 teaspoon ground cumin
1/2 teaspoon dried thyme
1/4 teaspoon salt
1/2 teaspoon black pepper
2 tablespoons butter
1/4 cup onion, finely minced
2 cloves garlic, minced
2 cans (15 ounces) tomato sauce
1 cup chicken stock
2 tablespoons brown sugar
1/2 tablespoon chipotle peppers in Adobo sauce, chopped
1 tablespoon unsweetened cocoa powder

In a small bowl combine all of the spices together including salt and pepper, mix well and set aside. In a large skillet melt the butter over medium heat. Add the onion and garlic, cook until the onions are soft. Stir in the mixture of spices, combine well and cook for 2 minutes. Stir in the tomato sauce and chicken stock; cook stirring occasionally for 10 minutes. Add brown sugar, chipotle peppers in Adobo sauce and cocoa powder. Stir until smooth, continue to cook on low heat for 5 minutes. Remove from heat and set aside until ready to use.

Note: If you like it a little spicier add more chipotle peppers in Adobo sauce or finely minced hot peppers of your choice.

Chicken Enchiladas:
2 pounds chicken tenders
1 1/2 teaspoons salt
2 teaspoons pepper
2 teaspoons paprika
2 teaspoons coriander
2 teaspoons chili powder
2 teaspoons ground cumin
2 teaspoons garlic powder
2 teaspoons onion powder
2 teaspoons oregano
1/2 teaspoon cayenne pepper
1/4 cup vegetable oil
1 small onion, finely chopped
2 tablespoons garlic, minced
1 yellow bell pepper, finely chopped
1 red bell pepper, finely chopped
1 1/2 cups chicken stock
8 (8 inch) corn or flour tortillas
2 cups cheddar cheese, shredded
1/4 cup cilantro, finely chopped (for garnish)
Other garnish suggestions: black olives, green onions, avocado, guacamole, salsa and sour cream

Preheat oven to 350 degrees and prepare a 13x9x2 inch baking dish with cooking spray and set aside.

Wash and thoroughly dry the chicken with paper towels. Combine the salt, pepper and all of the above spices in a small bowl; mix well. Season both sides of the chicken with the spices. Add the oil to a large skillet and heat on medium to medium high heat. When the oil is hot add the chicken and sauté to a golden brown on each side. Remove the chicken from the skillet once it is cooked through and set aside. Drain off any excess oil in the pan and discard. Add the onions, garlic and peppers; cook until vegetables are soft. Add the chicken stock and stir to loosen any bits at the bottom of the skillet. Simmer on low until liquid has reduced by half. Shred the chicken by pulling apart with two forks and add to the onion and pepper mixture, stir to combine. Add about 1/2 cup of Mole sauce to the bottom of the prepared baking dish and set aside. Wrap tortillas in aluminum foil and heat in oven for 10 minutes. When the tortillas are heated through add a generous 1/2 cup of the chicken mixture on the center of each tortilla; fold over and tuck in the ends. Place each rolled tortilla in the baking dish seam side down and finish by topping with Mole sauce and cheese. Cover with foil and heat in oven for about 20 minutes, uncover and heat for another 20 minutes or until heated through and cheese is melted. Garnish with chopped cilantro and any other garnish of choice.

Serves 6 to 8

Guess Who's Coming to Dinner

A new tradition began the first Thanksgiving that we celebrated in our newly built home by a very innocent mistake I made of buying a lofty and very healthy 26 pound turkey. We were quite proud of our latest endeavor and wanted to share our new home with a few friends and celebrate the holiday. It quickly became obvious that I was a little over zealous purchasing such a gigantic bird. I found it extremely difficult to manage this turkey, not to mention what happened when I could barely fit this beast in the oven because of its enormity! I fought and wrestled with this creature for most of the morning and I almost resorted to sitting on the floor and using my feet to push it in the oven. At one point I was sure I was going to lose the battle. Once I finally got it into the oven I felt like I was somewhere between giving birth and making a new friend. I decided then and there that something that had vied so hard for my attention deserved a name. After a family conference, a short debate and of course me catching my breath, we simply named it Joe. Naming the turkey was fun for our family, however for our guest listening to puzzling conversations all day about this apparently reclusive person which whom they seemed to think was in the house but had not met as of yet, was puzzling to say the least. Joe's name was mentioned on

and off throughout the day and unknowing to us our guest sometimes came to their own conclusions about our new friend Joe, as you will soon come to understand.
Myself: " Well, Joe is taken care of and he is finally dressed and ready to go".
Guest: Thinks to himself..."Who is Joe and where is he going"?
Husband: "How long will he need to be in"?
Guest: Thinks to himself..."What? Is this guy going to jail"?
Myself: "I think that damn turkey will be in for about 5 to 6. But don't worry about him, he's a tough old bird".
Guest: Thinks to himself..."I think they are talking about how many years he will be in the clinker".
Myself: "Geez, Joe is so heavy"!
Guest: Thinks to himself..."Well he must have put on a few pounds. It must be the stress".
Myself: Talking to my husband... "The next time I have to lift Joe I'm really going to need your help".
Guest: Thinks to himself..."Why is she lifting this guy and how old is he anyway"?
Husband: "Did you check Joe's temperature"?
Guest: Thinks to himself..."Great, let me get all of this straight. Joe is going to prison, he's fat, he's old, he has to be lifted and he's sick. What a great Thanksgiving this is going to be with this fat old jerk"!
Later in the afternoon the kids run into the kitchen after smelling the wonderful aromas all day and ask...."When is Joe going to be ready"?
Myself: "Only a little while longer. Joe is resting".
Guest. Thinks to himself..."What now? Are we really waiting for this guy to get up from a nap before we eat"?
A short while later when we were finally ready to serve the meal.
Guest: "Where is Joe going to sit"?
Myself: "Why I suppose we will place him at the head of the table with my husband".
Our guest looked perplexed over this long time friend of ours that he had never met. I then presented him with the silver platter that Joe so proudly lay upon and I said, "Meet Joe".
Our guest stood there looking confused and completely speechless! To this day we carry on the tradition of naming our Turkeys. You can name your bird if you like, but it may be a good idea to let your guest know who's coming to dinner. Or not!

Mexican Lasagna

Lasagna:
2 pounds lean ground beef
1/2 red onion, chopped
4 tablespoons Mexican seasoning (see recipe in section "Sauces and Seasonings")
2/3 cup water
1 jar (8 ounces) mild taco sauce
1 package (8 ounces) frozen corn
4 (8 inch) flour tortillas
1 can (16 ounces) refried beans
2 1/2 cups Queso Quesadilla cheese, shredded (creamy Mexican melting cheese)

Garnishes:
lettuce, shredded
green onions, chopped
cilantro, chopped
tomatoes, chopped
black olives, sliced
avocados, cut into bite size pieces
sour cream
hot sauce

Preheat oven to 425 degrees.

Prepare a square 2 quart baking dish with cooking spray and set aside.

In a large skillet over medium high heat add the ground beef and red onion. Cook stirring often while browning the meat and breaking into small bits. When the meat is cooked through remove from heat and drain off excess fat. Add the Mexican seasoning and the water to the meat and onion mixture. Cook over medium heat until the water is absorbed. Add the taco sauce and corn. Stir and continue to cook for 3 to 5 minutes. Remove from heat and set aside until ready to use.

Cut the tortillas into 3 inch wide strips resembling lasagna noodles. Spread each strip of tortillas with a thin layer of refried beans. In the prepared baking dish build the lasagna in layers of meat mixture, tortillas and shredded cheese. Repeat and finish with cheese on top.

Bake uncovered for 35 to 45 minutes or until the lasagna is heated through and the cheese is golden brown and bubbly. Cut into squares and serve with the garnishes of your choice.

Serves 6 to 8

Nana'a Lasagna

This is probably the most requested recipe of Nana's. Everyone is a big fan of her Lasagna!

Sauce:
2 tablespoons olive oil
1 medium onion, finely chopped
2 tablespoons garlic, minced
1 1/4 pounds ground beef, 85/15
1 beef bouillon cube
2 tablespoons Italian seasoning
1 bunch flat parsley, finely chopped
1/2 teaspoon salt
1 teaspoon pepper
3 cans (28 ounces each) crushed tomatoes

Heat the olive oil in a large skillet over medium high heat. Once the oil is hot add the onions and garlic; sauté until soft and translucent. Add the ground beef and cook until evenly browned. Drain off any extra fat from the beef if necessary. Reduce the heat to medium low and add the bouillon cube, Italian seasoning, parsley, salt and pepper; stir to combine.

Transfer the ground beef mixture to a large stock pot and add the crushed tomatoes. Bring to a gentle boil over medium high heat, once boiling turn the heat to a very low simmer. Cook for 1 hour. Cool completely and refrigerate overnight.

Lasagna:
1 package (1 pound) Lasagna noodles, about 12 noodles
1 egg, beaten
2 cups cottage cheese, small curd
2 cups mozzarella cheese, shredded and divided
2 cups Parmesan cheese, finely grated and divided
1/2 bunch parsley, finely chopped

Preheat oven to 400 degrees. Note: You will be turning the oven heat down to 350 degrees after the first 30 minutes of baking.

Cook the lasagna noodles according to the package directions. Once the noodles are cooked rinse under cold water to stop the cooking process, drain well and blot with a paper towel to remove any access moisture. Lay flat in a single layer on a cooking sheet until ready to assemble the lasagna.

Mix the beaten egg with the cottage cheese and set aside.

Layer the lasagna in a 13x9x2 baking dish.

Layers of lasagna as follows:
All of the following noodles are laid lengthwise.
1. Place a thin layer of the sauce in the bottom of the baking dish.
2. Add 3 noodles, generous sauce, mozzarella cheese and Parmesan cheese.
3. Add 3 noodles, cottage cheese mixture, mozzarella cheese, Parmesan cheese and chopped parsley.
4. Add 3 noodles, generous sauce, mozzarella cheese and Parmesan cheese.
5. Add 3 noodles, generous sauce and finish with Parmesan cheese.

Place the baking dish on a baking sheet that has been lined with aluminum foil. Cover the lasagna with foil that has been sprayed with cooking spray and bake in the oven for 30 minutes starting at 400 degrees. Reduce the oven to 350 degrees and cook an additional 30 minutes. Remove the foil during the last 10 minutes of baking. Let rest for 15 minutes before serving.

Nana's Tip: She suggests that you make the sauce the day before assembling the lasagna so the flavors can marry. Also add enough sauce to each layer so the noodles do not show through.

Serves 8 to 10

Side Dishes

Bread Stuffing

1 cup raisins
32 ounces cubed herb stuffing
1/2 cup butter
3 cups celery, finely chopped
3 cups onions, finely chopped
32 ounces chicken stock
2 teaspoons sage
1 teaspoon poultry seasoning
salt and pepper to taste
3 eggs, beaten

Preheat oven to 350 degrees. Prepare a 13x9x2 baking dish with cooking spray.

In a small bowl add the raisins and enough water to cover them. Let the raisins sit for at least two hours or more to rehydrate until they are plump. They may also be placed in the refrigerator overnight.

Add the cubed stuffing to a large bowl and set aside. Place the butter in a medium size skillet and heat on medium high heat. When the butter is hot add the chopped celery and onions; cook until soft and translucent. Add the stock to the vegetables and stir to combine. Remove from heat. Add the stock and vegetable mixture to the cubed stuffing. Add the sage, poultry seasoning, salt and pepper; mix well. Set aside to cool. When the mixture has cooled significantly add the beaten eggs and raisins; stir to combine. Add more chicken stock if needed. Mixture should be moist but not soupy. Pour mixture into the prepared baking dish. Bake covered with foil for 30 minutes. Remove foil and continue to cook for an additional 30 minutes. It is done when it is heated through the center and slightly toasted on top. Serve immediately.

Note: You may use this recipe for cornbread stuffing as well. Omit the raisins and substitute the cubed stuffing with 32 ounces of day old cornbread broken into crumbs.

Yield: Serves 8 to 10

Timbale is a method of cooking a creamy vegetable or meat mixture in a mold. It is also another term for a mold in which it is cooked. You can use individual ramekins, custard cups or french cocottes.

Carrots Timbale

2 pounds carrots, peeled and cut into 1 inch pieces
2 eggs, beaten
1 egg yolk, beaten
1/2 cup heavy cream
1/4 cup butter, melted and cooled
1/2 teaspoon nutmeg, freshly grated
salt to taste
Garnishes:
1/4 teaspoon ground cinnamon
1 tablespoon sugar
chopped pecans

Preheat oven to 425 degrees. Prepare 8 to 10 timbale molds with cooking spray and set aside.

In a large pot bring the carrots to a boil in salted water over medium high heat. Cook until the carrots are fork tender. Strain the carrots and let cool completely. Puree the carrots in a food processor until you have a fine but not soupy mixture. Add the eggs, heavy cream, melted butter, nutmeg and salt to taste; mix well. Add the filling to the prepared timbale molds. Place the filled timbale molds in a large roasting pan filled with simmering water. Water should be about halfway up to the top of the molds. Place in oven and cook for 50 minutes.

In a small bowl combine the ground cinnamon and sugar together. Garnish the Timbale's with the ground cinnamon sugar mixture and chopped pecans. Serve hot.

Yield: Serves 8 to 10

Every summer we enjoy our upstate New York locally grown corn. We have many corn farms that grace the beautiful area around us and we always enjoy a corn run to the local "Honor Box" to buy this just picked treat. The farmers are all very trusting in their customers because they don't always man the stands. You pick out your corn, leave the money in the honor box, make your own change and hop in your car and go! How refreshing is that? All season I collect the uneaten cooked ears and freeze them. Typically around Labor Day I like to make a big batch of creamed corn. It's our last taste of that wonderful fresh corn we had for the season!

Creamed Corn

1/2 cup butter
8 cups fresh corn, cooked and removed from cobs
2 tablespoons all purpose flour
1/2 cup whole milk
2 cups heavy cream
salt and pepper to taste

In a large skillet melt the butter over medium heat. When the foam has subsided add the corn to the skillet and stir. In a small bowl combine the flour and whole milk. Whisk until you have a smooth slurry. Add the slurry to the corn and stir. Add the heavy cream. Add salt and pepper to taste. Continue to simmer until it has thickened to a creamy consistency. You can adjust the milk to more or less as needed.

Note: I like to use my bundt pan when I'm removing the kernels from the cob. The cob is secure in the center hole and the kernels fall very neatly in the well of the pan.

Yield: Serves 8

Fried Green Tomatoes

4 green tomatoes (cored and sliced into 1/2 inch thick slices)
3 tablespoons Cajun seasoning, (see recipe in section "Sauces and Seasonings")
2 eggs
1 teaspoon black pepper, divided
1 1/2 cups unseasoned bread crumbs
1 1/2 cups yellow cornmeal
1 tablespoon salt
1/2 teaspoon onion powder
1/2 teaspoon cayenne pepper
1/2 cup vegetable oil, divided
1 cup Parmesan cheese
1 cup Buttermilk Ranch Dressing (see recipe in section "Salads and Dressings")

Preheat oven to 200 degrees.

Remove the core and slice the tomatoes. Place between paper towels and dry. Sprinkle generously with Cajun seasoning on both sides and set aside.

Whisk together eggs and a pinch of black pepper in an 8 inch pie plate. In another 8 inch pie plate combine the bread crumbs, cornmeal, salt, onion powder, cayenne pepper and the rest of the black pepper. Dip the tomato slices in the egg mixture and then in the bread crumb mixture. Place on a baking sheet lined with parchment paper and place in refrigerator for 30 minutes or more to set.

In a heavy skillet heat 1/4 cup of the vegetable oil until hot over medium high heat. Place tomatoes in skillet without crowding them. Cook for 2 to 3 minutes on each side or until brown. Avoid turning more than once. When cooking second batch you may need to add additional oil, if so make sure the oil is heated again before adding more tomatoes.

Drain the tomatoes on a paper towel as they cook. After they are drained put them on an oven proof platter to keep warm in the oven until all of the tomatoes are fried. Just before serving sprinkle with Parmesan cheese and serve with Buttermilk Ranch Dressing on the side.

Yield: Serves 4 to 6

LAKE
LIFE

Macaroni and Cheese

1 pound elbow macaroni, uncooked
1 tablespoon salt
2 tablespoons cornstarch
1/2 teaspoon Coleman's dry mustard
1/8 teaspoon nutmeg, freshly grated
1/8 teaspoon cayenne pepper
1 teaspoon salt
1/4 teaspoon pepper
2 1/2 cups milk
2 tablespoons butter
1 cup sharp cheddar cheese, shredded
1 cup fontina cheese, shredded
3/4 cup Roasted Garlic Croutons, optional (see recipe in section "Salads and Dressings")

Preheat oven to 375 degrees. Prepare a 2 quart baking dish with cooking spray and set aside.

In a large saucepan over medium high heat add 4 cups of water and 1 tablespoon of salt, bring to a boil and add macaroni. Boil for about 9 minutes or until elbows are al dente. Do not overcook. Drain and rinse in colander with cool water to stop cooking process. Drain well and set aside.

In a medium saucepan (removed from heat) combine cornstarch, dry mustard, nutmeg, cayenne pepper, salt and pepper. Over low heat slowly add milk while stirring with a whisk to remove any lumps. Add butter and continue to stir constantly. Bring to a gentle simmer over medium low heat and continue to cook until thickened; remove from heat. In a separate bowl combine cheeses together. Add 1 3/4 cups of cheese to the saucepan, reserving 1/4 for later; stir until melted. Combine the cooked macaroni and the cheese and milk mixture; gently fold together. Pour macaroni and cheese mixture into the prepared baking dish. Sprinkle with reserved cheese. Top with Roasted Garlic Croutons if desired. Bake uncovered for 30 to 40 minutes or until lightly golden and bubbling.

Serve hot.

Yield: Serves 6

Just picked from the garden!

Sautéed Collard Greens

3 large bunches collard greens (about 3 pounds)
1/4 cup olive oil
1/2 pound bacon, cut into 1 inch pieces
1/2 stick of butter
1 medium onion, chopped
4 cloves garlic, finely chopped
1 1/2 cups chicken stock
salt and pepper

Prepare collard greens by cleaning them thoroughly. Remove the thick stems and stack several leaves on top of each other and roll like a cigar. Cut leaves into 1 inch slices. Repeat until all leaves are cut and set aside.

Heat the olive oil in a very large skillet or braising pan (I use an 18 quart braising pan) over medium to medium high heat. Add the bacon and cook until the fat is rendered out. Add the butter and heat until hot and the foam has subsided. Add the onion and garlic; sauté until the onion is soft and translucent. Add the collard greens and stir constantly as greens are wilting and cooking down. Slowly and as needed add the chicken stock. Add salt and pepper to taste and continue to cook for 15 minutes or so until the greens are tender. You may need to adjust with more stock or butter as needed.

Yield: Serves 4 to 6

Stuffed Herb Tomatoes

6 medium tomatoes, ripe
kosher salt
fresh ground pepper
1 1/2 tablespoons garlic, minced
3 tablespoons green onions, minced
2 tablespoons fresh basil, minced
2 tablespoons fresh parsley, minced
1/2 teaspoon thyme
1/4 cup olive oil
1/2 cup Roasted Garlic Croutons, crumbled (see recipe in section "Salads and Dressings")
1/2 cup Parmesan cheese

Preheat oven to 400 degrees.

Remove the stems and cut the tomatoes into half crosswise. Gently press out the juice and seeds. Sprinkle the tomatoes lightly with salt and pepper; set aside.

Mix all of the ingredients together in a mixing bowl. Fill each tomato with the mixture. Sprinkle with Parmesan cheese. Place on a baking sheet and bake for 15 to 20 minutes or until the tomatoes are cooked through.

Serve hot.

Yield: Serves 6

Sugar Snap Peas in Pancetta and Balsamic Vinegar

1 jar (2 ounces) pine nuts
8 ounces Italian pancetta
3 cups fresh sugar snap peas
1/4 cup balsamic vinegar
2 tablespoons sugar
salt and pepper to taste

Preheat oven to 375 degrees.

Place the pine nuts on a baking sheet and place in the oven. While watching carefully bake for 5 minutes or until pine nuts are golden in color. Remove from the oven and set aside.

Wash the peas and remove tough string by cutting one end and pulling the string off that is on the inside curve of the pea.

Cook the pancetta in a large skillet over medium high heat until the fat has rendered out and the pancetta is just beginning to crisp, about 5 minutes. Remove the pancetta with a slotted spoon and set aside leaving any fat in the skillet. Add the sugar snap peas and toss to coat with the fat. Cook and stir until just cooked through, about 3 to 5 minutes. Add the balsamic vinegar, sugar and pancetta. Continue cooking until the balsamic vinegar has reduced and the sugar is dissolved, about 2 minutes. Season to taste with salt and pepper. Add the pine nuts and toss to combine. Serve immediately.

Note: You can also use Brussel Sprouts instead of sugar snap peas. Wash the Brussel Sprouts thoroughly and remove any unsightly leaves. Slice off bottom stem, half each sprout lengthwise and cook just as you would the peas. The Brussel Sprouts will take about 10 minutes to cook until they are tender.

Yield: Serves 4

Meet
Us
at
The
Chestnut Inn
...On Oquaga Lake!
Where Delightful Folks Meet and Drink!

Zucchini and Summer Squash Bake

1/2 cup olive oil, divided
1 large onion, minced
2 cloves garlic, minced
1 pound (1 large or 2 small) zucchini
1 pound (1 large or 2 small) yellow summer squash
2 tablespoons fresh thyme, minced
2 tablespoons fresh oregano, minced
salt and pepper to taste
1 pound roasted tomatoes (see recipe in this section "Side Dishes")
1 1/4 cups Parmesan cheese, grated

Preheat oven to 350 degrees. Prepare a shallow 2 quart baking dish with cooking spray and set aside.

In a medium skillet heat 3 tablespoons of olive oil over medium heat. Add the onions and garlic; sauté until soft. Spread the onions and garlic evenly in the bottom of the prepared shallow baking dish.

Cut the zucchini and squash into 1/4 inch slices on the bias. In a medium size bowl toss the zucchini and squash with 3 tablespoons of the olive oil, thyme, oregano, salt and pepper.

Alternating between zucchini and squash place them standing on their sides in the baking dish. Place tomatoes between every 3 or 4 pieces of zucchini and squash; filling in evenly until all of the tomatoes are used.

Sprinkle entire dish with grated Parmesan cheese and bake covered with aluminum foil for 35 minutes. Remove foil and finish baking for an additional 35 minutes or until bubbling and the vegetables are tender. Let cool for 15 minutes before serving.

Serves 8

Applesauce

3 to 4 pounds apples, peeled, cored and quartered, (about 12 medium apples)
Cortland, Golden Delicious or Jonathan varieties
4 strips lemon peel
juice of 1 lemon
2 cinnamon sticks
1/4 cup dark brown sugar
1/4 cup sugar
1 cup water
1/2 teaspoon salt

Place all of the ingredients into a large stockpot. Cover and bring to a boil over medium high heat. Lower heat and simmer on low for 30 minutes or until apples are tender and falling apart. Remove from heat. Remove lemon peels and cinnamon sticks. Mash apples with a potato masher. Serve hot or cool to room temperature and refrigerate. Applesauce can be frozen up to 6 months. Makes about two quarts.

Yield: Serves 8

Country Green Beans

1 pound fresh green beans
1 cup chicken or beef stock
1/2 cup shallots, chopped
2 slices bacon, cooked
salt and pepper
1 tablespoon parsley, minced

Wash the beans, trim the ends, remove the string and cut in half crosswise. Combine the beans, stock, shallots, bacon, salt and pepper in a saucepan. Bring to a boil over medium high heat. Lower heat to a simmer, cover and cook for about 20 minutes or until beans are tender, stirring occasionally. Garnish with parsley and serve.

Yield: Serves 6

Creamed Collard Greens

4 large bunches collard greens (about 4 pounds)
salt and pepper
1/2 stick butter
3 shallots, chopped
2 cloves garlic, chopped
2 cups heavy cream
1 teaspoon fresh nutmeg, grated
1 cup Parmesan cheese, grated
salt and pepper

Clean the collard greens thoroughly. Remove the thick tough stems. Stack several leaves on top of each other a few at a time and roll cigar style. Cut into 2 inch pieces. Add enough salted water to a stock pot to cover the greens and bring to a boil. Cook for about 20 minutes or until the greens are tender. Drain in a colander and set aside.

In a large skillet melt the butter, add the shallots and garlic; sauté until tender. Turn the heat to low and slowly add the heavy cream while stirring constantly. Add the nutmeg and Parmesan cheese. Continue to stir until the sauce is thickened. Add drained collard greens and heat through. Season to taste with salt and pepper.

Yield: Serves 6 to 8

Creamed Spinach

2 packages (10 ounces each) frozen spinach, chopped
2 tablespoons butter
1/4 cup shallots, finely chopped
2 tablespoons garlic, minced
2 cups cream cheese, room temperature
1/2 cup sour cream, room temperature
2 cups Parmesan cheese, grated
salt and freshly ground pepper to taste

Several hours before cooking thaw the spinach in a colander, drain and press to remove as much water as possible. The spinach needs to be completely thawed and drained before you can assemble this dish.

In a medium saucepan melt the butter over medium heat. When the foam has subsided add the shallots and sauté for 2 minutes. Add the garlic and sauté for another 2 minutes. Add the spinach, cream cheese, sour cream and Parmesan cheese. Heat through and stir to combine; add salt and pepper to taste. Turn the heat to a low simmer to keep warm. Do not overcook. Serve immediately.

Yield: Serves 6 to 8

Crispy Potato Wedges

2 pounds small red potatoes
1/2 cup olive oil
1 1/2 tablespoons whole grain Dijon mustard
3 tablespoons garlic, minced
1/2 tablespoon paprika
1/2 tablespoon thyme
course sea salt
fresh ground pepper
1 1/2 tablespoons fresh parsley, chopped

Preheat oven to 400 degrees.

Wash the potatoes and cut into fourths. Combine the oil, mustard and garlic in a large bowl. Add the potatoes and toss to coat well. Sprinkle liberally with paprika, thyme, sea salt and pepper; toss again.

Spread the potatoes on a baking sheet and bake for 45 minutes or until the potatoes are crispy on the outside and fork tender.

Sprinkle with the fresh parsley before serving.

Serve hot.

Yield: Serves 8

Mexican Rice

1/4 cup vegetable oil
1 1/2 cups white rice
1 medium onion, minced
1 medium green bell pepper, minced
1/2 jalapeño pepper, seeded and chopped
2 tablespoons garlic, minced
1 can (10 ounces) Rotel Tomatoes
3 tablespoons of chipotle peppers in Adobo sauce, finely chopped
juice of 1 lime
1 tablespoon Tabasco sauce
2 tablespoons fresh parsley, minced
2 tablespoons cilantro, minced
1 teaspoon cumin
3 cups water
2 teaspoons salt
1/2 teaspoon pepper
1 cup sharp cheddar cheese, grated

In a 2 quart dutch oven or stock pot add the vegetable oil and heat over medium high heat. Once the oil is hot add the rice and sauté over medium to medium high heat until golden brown. Add the onion, green bell pepper, jalapeño pepper and garlic; continue to cook until the vegetables are soft. Add the remaining ingredients except for the cheese. Bring to a gentle boil and immediately reduce the heat to a low simmer and cover with a tight fitting lid. Do not lift the lid! Continue to cook for 20 minutes. Remove from heat and keep the pot covered while letting the rice rest for about 5 minutes. Fluff with a fork.

Just before serving fold the cheese into the hot rice and gently combine until melted. Serve hot.

Yield: Serves 8 to 10

Potatoes Gratin

2 tablespoons butter
1/2 pound bacon, cut into 1 inch pieces
1/2 medium onion, finely chopped
4 medium russet potatoes, peeled and sliced thin
salt and pepper
1/2 cup heavy cream
1/2 cup chicken stock
1 cup cheddar cheese, shredded
1 cup Gruyere cheese, shredded
1/4 cup fresh parsley, chopped

Preheat oven to 375 degrees.

Butter the sides and bottom of a 2 quart baking dish and set aside.

Fry the bacon in a medium size skillet over medium high heat until just crisp. Once the bacon is cooked remove it from the skillet with a slotted spoon and set aside on paper towels to drain. Pour out all but two tablespoons of the bacon grease and add the onions. Sauté the onions until they are soft and translucent. Remove from heat and set aside. Layer the potatoes in the prepared baking dish, sprinkling each layer with salt and pepper. Mix the cream and stock together in a small bowl and pour over the potatoes. Sprinkle the onion and bacon on top of the potatoes.

Cover with foil and bake for 30 minutes. Remove foil and continue to bake for another 30 minutes or until the potatoes are tender. Sprinkle with cheese and broil just long enough for cheese to melt while watching very closely. Garnish with the fresh parsley just before serving.

Serve hot.

Yield: Serves 6

Roasted Tomatoes

Oh, what to do with all of those spectacular tomatoes that grow in your garden all summer long? It seems like they all come to fruition about the same time and you just absolutely can't bare to let one single tomato go to waste! One particular summer we had an amazing crop that was plentiful and each tomato was prettier than the next. Thank goodness for this recipe because it saved the day. I roasted hundreds of tomatoes and froze them. We finished the last container of tomatoes on a cold snowy day eating hot pasta with Bill's Italian Tomato Sauce (see recipe in section "Main Dishes"). All the while it reminded us of summer at the cottage!

12 to 24 ripe tomatoes
olive oil

Preheat oven to 200 degrees.

Wash tomatoes and cut off the stem end. Halve the tomatoes lengthwise and then quarter. The goal is to have all of the tomatoes uniformly about the same size. Place them on a baking sheet. Drizzle with olive oil and gently toss to coat well, turning them skin side down to bake.

Bake for 2 to 3 hours. You can't go wrong cooking them the longer amount of time. Let cool completely before removing them from the baking sheet.

Place them in an airtight container and refrigerate for up to a week or place in freezer bags for 6 months.

You can also eat the tomatoes right off of the baking sheet with a piece of crusty bread, use for a simple salad, eat on a burger, in soups and stews, over pasta or puree in blender for a rich tomato sauce.

Yield: Serves 6

Scalloped Potatoes

4 tablespoons butter
2 tablespoons all purpose flour
2 cups milk
1 teaspoon salt
fresh ground pepper to taste
1 tablespoon garlic powder
4 medium potatoes, peeled and thinly sliced
1 medium onion, chopped
24 ounces cheddar cheese, grated

Preheat oven to 350 degrees. Prepare a 13x9x2 inch baking dish with cooking spray and set aside.

In a large skillet over medium heat melt the butter. Slowly add the flour and stir to combine until mixture becomes a smooth paste. Continue to cook for a few minutes more while stirring constantly until you have a very light golden color. Slowly add the milk while stirring until it is a creamy consistency. Season with salt, pepper and garlic powder. Continue cooking and stirring until mixture thickens and starts to simmer very gently. Taste for seasonings. Remove from heat and set aside.

In the baking dish, layer in potatoes, onions, white sauce and cheese. Continue adding layers until baking dish is full. Top the final layer with cheese. Bake covered with foil for 45 minutes, uncover and bake for an additional 30 minutes or until potatoes are fork tender.

Serve hot.

Yield: Serves 8

Southern Rice

The first important staples that my sisters and I learned to cook were sweet tea and white rice. I believe that every southern child must know how to prepare these items as they're consumed on a daily basis. While both of these are easy to prepare, they must be perfected in quality otherwise the whole house will be upset with you.

2 cups water
2 teaspoons salt
1 cup long grain white rice

Add the water, salt and rice in a medium saucepan; cook on medium high heat until boiling. Once the rice is boiling immediately reduce the heat to a very low simmer. Cover the saucepan with a tight fitting lid and cook for 20 minutes. DO NOT LIFT THE LID while cooking! Let the rice rest for 5 to 10 minutes and fluff with a fork.
Serve hot.

Yield: Serves 4 to 6

Sunday Grits

4 1/2 cups water
1 teaspoon salt
1 cup uncooked grits (not instant)
1/2 cup butter
1 tablespoon garlic, minced
12 ounces cheddar cheese, grated
1/2 cup whole milk
2 eggs, beaten and room temperature

Preheat oven to 350 degrees.

Prepare a 2 quart baking dish with cooking spray and set aside.

Bring the water and salt to a boil in a 2 quart saucepan. Slowly add in the grits. Reduce the heat to medium low and stir. Cook for about 7 minutes or until thickened, stirring constantly. Add the butter, garlic and cheese; continue to stir constantly until the cheese is melted. Turn off the heat and cool slightly. Warm the milk in the microwave (NOT HOT). Add the room temperature eggs to a small bowl and beat well. Slowly add the warm milk to the eggs while whisking constantly. Slowly add the milk and egg mixture to the grits and continue to stir until combined.

Pour into the prepared 2 quart baking dish and bake for about 35 minutes or until heated through completely.

Yield: Serves 8 to 10

Sweet Potato Casserole

6 medium sweet potatoes
1/2 cup dark brown sugar
1/2 teaspoon cinnamon
1/4 teaspoon ground cloves
1/4 teaspoon nutmeg
1 teaspoon vanilla extract
1/2 cup butter
1/2 cup heavy cream
2 eggs, beaten
1/2 cup chopped pecans, optional
24 large marshmallows

In advance of assembling the casserole wrap the potatoes in aluminum foil and place on a foil lined baking sheet. Bake in the oven at 350 degrees for about 1 to 1 1/2 hours or until fork tender. You can bake the potatoes the day before, cool completely and refrigerate overnight.

Preheat oven to 350 degrees. Prepare a 3 quart baking dish with cooking spray and set aside.

Remove the skins from the potatoes. Add the baked potatoes, brown sugar, cinnamon, cloves, nutmeg, vanilla extract, butter and heavy cream to a large mixing bowl. Start on low speed with an electric mixer to combine. Add the eggs and raise the speed to medium high for 2 or 3 minutes until fluffy and well incorporated. Important note: If the potatoes are hot let the mixture cool completely before adding the eggs.

Place the potato mixture into the prepared three quart baking dish and top with pecans and marshmallows. Loosely cover with foil and bake for 30 minutes. Remove foil and bake for 30 minutes more or until marshmallows are golden brown and casserole is heated through.

Serve hot.

Yield: Serves 12

Caribbean Fried Plantains

2 plantains, ripe (black in color)
1/4 cup vegetable oil

Peel and slice the plantains on a diagonal.

Heat the oil in a medium size skillet over medium heat. When the oil is hot add the plantains to the skillet in a single layer without crowding them. Fry until golden brown on each side. Drain on paper towels. Serve while hot.

Note: Never refrigerate plantains.

Yield: Serves 4

Creamy Polenta

4 1/2 cups half and half
1 cup polenta
3 tablespoons sugar
salt and pepper to taste

In a medium saucepan bring the half and half to a soft boil over medium heat, stirring constantly. Reduce the heat to low and slowly add the polenta, sugar, salt and pepper. Mix thoroughly and remove from heat. Serve while hot.

Yield: Serves 8

Breads

Banana Bread

1 1/2 sticks butter, melted and cooled
2 cups all purpose flour
1 1/2 teaspoons baking soda
1/2 teaspoon salt
1 teaspoon cinnamon
1/2 teaspoon ground nutmeg
4 overripe bananas, divided
1 cup sugar
2 large eggs
1 teaspoon vanilla extract

Preheat oven to 350 degrees. Lightly grease a 9x5 inch loaf pan and set aside.

In a small bowl melt the butter in the microwave and set aside to cool.

In a large bowl combine the flour, baking soda, salt, cinnamon and nutmeg; set aside.

Lightly mash 2 of the bananas with a fork in a small bowl and set aside. Whip the remaining bananas and sugar together with an electric mixer on medium speed until you get a fluffy banana cream. Add the melted butter, eggs and vanilla extract; beat well. Mix in the dry ingredients just until incorporated; do not over mix. Gently fold in the mashed banana.

Pour the batter into the prepared loaf pan. Bake for 1 hour and 15 minutes or until a toothpick inserted into the center of the loaf comes out clean.

Cool the bread in the pan for 10 to 15 minutes. Turn onto a wire rack to cool completely before slicing.

Yield: Serves 8 to 10

Our holiday meals would never be the same without these wonderful rolls made by our friend Alexis! She very generously gave me the recipe and it's a keeper!

Refrigerator Rolls

1 cup shortening, melted
1 cup sugar
1 1/2 teaspoons salt
1 cup boiling water
2 eggs, lightly beaten
2 packages dry yeast
1 cup warm water
6 cups flour
1 1/2 tablespoons vegetable oil

Combine the melted shortening, sugar, salt and boiling water. Let mixture cool completely. Add the beaten eggs.

Sprinkle the yeast into the warm water. Allow to sit for 5 to 10 minutes; stir gently to combine. Add the yeast and water mixture to the shortening mixture. Gradually add the flour and mix completely.

Place the dough in an oiled bowl, turning to coat with the oil. Cover the bowl with plastic wrap and then a damp tea towel. Store in the refrigerator for at least 4 hours or overnight.

Two to three hours before serving, remove the dough from the refrigerator and punch down. Pinch off pieces of the dough and roll into small balls about half the size of a well in a muffin tin. Place each ball into the wells of 3 greased muffin tins and cover with a dry cloth. Allow to rise in a warm place away from drafts for 1 to 2 hours.

Preheat oven to 350 degrees.

Bake for 20 to 25 minutes or until nicely golden brown. Serve while hot. Makes 36 rolls.

Yield: Serves 16 to 18

Buttermilk Biscuits

2 cups all purpose flour
1 tablespoon baking powder
1/2 teaspoon baking soda
1/2 teaspoon salt
6 tablespoons vegetable shortening, cold and cut into small pieces
1 cup buttermilk
2 tablespoons butter, melted

Preheat oven to 450 degrees.

In a large mixing bowl add the flour, baking powder, baking soda and salt. Whisk together to combine. Cut in the vegetable shortening with a pastry cutter. Slowly stir in the buttermilk and mix well to combine with all of the dry ingredients. The dough should be just so ever slightly sticky. Turn the dough out onto a lightly floured surface and knead only 3 to 4 times. If the dough is too sticky pat a very small amount of flour onto the dough and on your hands. Be aware that over mixing and over kneading the dough will cause you to have tough biscuits. With a floured rolling pin roll out the dough on the floured surface to 3/4 inch thickness. Cut the biscuits out with a 2 inch biscuit cutter and place on a baking sheet about 1/2 inch apart. Gather the scraps and pat into another small mound, roll out and cut out any remaining dough. Lightly brush the tops with melted butter. Bake until the biscuits are lightly golden brown on top, about 12 to 15 minutes. Makes about 12 biscuits.

Yield: Serves 6

Classic Cream Scones

2 cups flour
2 teaspoons baking powder
4 tablespoons sugar, divided
1/2 teaspoon salt
4 tablespoons butter, cold
2 eggs, beaten
1/2 cup heavy cream, plus 1 tablespoon
1/2 cup dried cranberries
zest of 1/2 lemon

Preheat oven to 425 degrees.

Spray a baking sheet with cooking spray and set aside.

Mix the flour, baking powder, 2 tablespoons of the sugar and salt in a large bowl; stir to combine. With a pastry cutter work in the butter until you have a mixture that resembles coarse meal. Add the eggs and 1/2 cup of heavy cream, stir until blended. Very gently fold in the cranberries and lemon zest.

Turn the dough out onto a lightly floured surface and knead about 5 times. With a floured rolling pin roll the dough out in a circular shape that is about 3/4 inch thick and cut into 12 wedges. Place the wedges on the prepared cookie sheet. Combine 2 tablespoons of the sugar and 1 tablespoon of the heavy cream together in a small bowl and brush on top of the wedges. Bake for about 15 minutes or until lightly golden brown.

Yield: Makes 12 scones

Dumplings

2 cups all purpose flour
1 tablespoon baking powder
1/2 teaspoon salt
3 tablespoons butter, room temperature
1 cup whole milk

In a medium size bowl combine the flour, baking powder and salt together and mix well with a whisk. Cut in the butter with a pastry cutter or a fork. Slowly add the milk while stirring.

With floured hands roll the dough into balls about the size of golf balls. Gently flatten each ball into about 1/2 inch thickness.

Drop the dumplings carefully into hot liquid and occasionally ladle over the dumplings. Simmer for about ten minutes uncovered and another 10 minutes covered or until dumplings are cooked through in the center.

Note: See the recipes for Chicken and Dumplings under "Soups and Stews" and Blueberry Dumplings under "Desserts".

Yield: Makes 8 to 10 dumplings.

Mexican Corn Bread

1 1/2 cups yellow corn meal
1 teaspoon salt
3 teaspoons baking powder
2 eggs, beaten
2/3 cup vegetable oil
1 cup sour cream
2 tablespoons jalapeños (jarred), chopped
1 jar (8 ounces) pimientos
1 can (15 ounces) cream corn
1 cup cheddar cheese, grated

Preheat oven to 350 degrees. Prepare an 8 inch square baking pan with cooking spray and set aside.

Combine the corn meal, salt, and baking powder; mix well. Add eggs, oil and sour cream; stir until mixture is just blended. Stir in jalapeños, pimientos, corn and cheese. Pour the batter into the prepared 8 inch square baking pan. Bake for 35 to 40 minutes or until lightly browned. Let cool and cut into squares.

Yield: Serves 6 to 8

Tina's Beer Rolls

This is a simple recipe with many good memories! I remember enjoying these muffins during my high school years at the home of my girlfriend, Tina. I always looked forward to joining her family for dinner because her Mom was so nice and her Dad was very funny (minus the lectures). After dinner, Tina and I always cleaned up the kitchen and hand washed the dishes. We made it a fun chore together as we laughed and talked about boys! I almost always think of her to this day when I have my hands in a sink of warm sudsy water! I can still feel her standing beside me and it makes me happy as I laugh to myself.

3 cups Bisquick
3 tablespoons sugar
1 can beer (not light)

Preheat oven to 400 degrees. Prepare a muffin tin with cooking spray and set aside.

Mix all of the ingredients together in a medium size bowl and pour into the prepared muffin tin. Bake for 25 minutes or until muffins are lightly golden brown. Makes 12 muffins.

Yield: Serves 6 to 8

Yorkshire Pudding

4 large eggs (measured in a measuring cup)
equal quantity of milk to eggs
pinch of salt
equal quantity of all purpose flour to eggs
1/4 cup vegetable oil

Preheat oven to 450 degrees.

Pour the eggs and milk into the pitcher of an electric blender; add the salt. Mix thoroughly and let stand for 10 minutes.

Gradually add the flour to the milk and egg mixture; blend until you have a lump free batter.

Leave the batter to rest for 30 minutes or longer. You can also keep it up to several hours in the refrigerator.

Place 1 teaspoon of vegetable oil into each well of a muffin tin. Heat the muffin tin in the oven until the oil is hot and just smoking. Carefully remove the hot muffin tin from the oven. Blend the batter one last time. While the oil is still hot fill the wells with the batter about halfway full.

Place in the oven and bake for about 20 minutes or until puffy and golden brown.

Best served with Prime Rib Roast of Beef (see recipe in section "Main Dishes").

Yield: Serves 12

Desserts

This recipe was a childhood favorite of ours during the summer! We often picked fresh figs in our backyard in Tennessee. Here in upstate New York it's blueberries! You can make this recipe with almost any fruit. Blueberries, figs and peaches are at the top of my list!

Blueberry Dumplings

2 quarts fresh blueberries
1/2 cup sugar
1 1/2 cups water
dumplings (see recipe in section "Breads")
1 quart vanilla ice cream

Wash and pick over the blueberries, removing any stems and bad berries; drain well. In a medium size bowl toss the fruit gently while adding the sugar to coat. Add the blueberries and the water to a large pot. Cook on medium heat until the blueberries become just a bit soupy and a soft boil begins. Reduce the heat to a low simmer.

Meanwhile follow the directions for making the dumplings. Drop the dumplings carefully into the gently simmering blueberries. Ladle the hot liquid over the dumplings. Reduce the heat and cook uncovered for 10 minutes, cover and cook an additional 10 minutes or until the dumplings are cooked through in the center. Serve hot with a scoop of vanilla ice cream.

Note: You can adjust the sweetness by adding more or less sugar. You may also adjust the consistency by adding more or less water.

Yield: Serves 6

I have many fond memories of "Ice Box Pies" growing up in Memphis, Tennessee. No one in Memphis had better Ice Box Pies than the Buntyn Cafe' on Southern Avenue. Their pies were two stories high! All of the waitresses were older and had worked there for most of their adult lives. I seem to recall that you had to wait for one of the waitresses to pass on before you could get a job there and you still had to wait longer because they passed those jobs down in their families. Each waitress was unique but they all had one thing in common; their hair! It was either "Old Lady Blue" or what I call "Waitress Black". It was so black it was blue!

Chocolate Ice Box Pie

Crust:
20 chocolate sandwich cookies, inside cream removed
1/4 cup butter, melted
Filling:
1 cup sugar
3 tablespoons cornstarch
1/3 cup flour
1/4 teaspoon kosher salt
1/8 teaspoon cinnamon
1 cup chocolate chips
3 cups milk
3 large egg yolks, room temperature
1 tablespoon vanilla extract
Topping:
sweetened whip cream

Crust:
Crumble the cookies into the bowl of a food processor and process to crumbs. You should have about two cups. Place the crumbs in a bowl and mix in the melted butter. Press the crumbs evenly over the bottom and up the sides of a 9 inch pie pan. Chill in the refrigerator until needed.

Filling:
Sift the sugar, cornstarch, flour, salt and cinnamon together into a medium size bowl; set aside. Combine the chocolate chips and milk in a sauce pan; cook over medium heat while stirring constantly. As soon as the chips are melted pull the pan off of the heat and pour half of the chocolate mixture into the dry ingredients; mix well. Whisk the egg yolks and vanilla together in a separate bowl; set side. Let the chocolate mixture that is remaining in the saucepan cool. Once it has cooled completely add the egg yolks and vanilla extract; stir to combine. Add the chocolate mixture combined with the dry ingredients back into the saucepan and stir. Set the saucepan back over medium high heat and whisk aggressively. Once the mixture starts to thicken keep whisking and cooking for 2 minutes. Pour the chocolate filling into a bowl and cool for 10 minutes. Once it has cooled pour the mixture into the pie shell and level the top. Chill for several hours in the refrigerator. Generously top the pie with sweetened whipped cream. Serve cold.

Yield: Serves 6 to 8

During the course of building our home I often made these cookies for all of the wonderful people who worked on the construction site. This recipe makes about 7 dozen or so, just enough to satisfy the many people that it took to do the job! Each time I visited the project site I "whipped" up a batch and carted them along. The workers were always happy to see these cookies coming and the entire batch was usually finished by the end of the day!

Construction Worker Cookies

2 cups butter
2 cups sugar
2 cups brown sugar
4 eggs
2 teaspoons vanilla extract
4 cups flour
5 cups oatmeal, quick cooking
1 teaspoon salt
2 teaspoons baking powder
2 teaspoons baking soda

Variations:
chocolate chips
nuts
coconut, shredded
peanut butter chips
raisins
cranberries, dried
cherries, dried

Preheat oven to 350 degrees.

With an electric mixer on medium speed cream together the butter, sugar and brown sugar. With the electric mixer still running add the eggs one at a time and the vanilla extract. Mix on low speed to blend thoroughly.

In a separate bowl whisk together the flour, oatmeal, salt, baking powder and baking soda. Slowly add the dry ingredients 1/2 cup at a time into the butter and sugar mixture; mix until completely blended.

Fold in chocolate chips, nuts or any variation listed above or all of the above.

Place golf ball size scoops of dough on cookie sheets. Do not overcrowd the cookies. Bake for 12 minutes or until edges are golden brown. Do not over bake. The cookies will still be light in color when they are removed from the oven. Let the cookies rest for about 3 minutes and gently transfer onto baking racks to cool.

Yield: Makes 7 to 8 dozen

One of my fondest memories as a little girl, was my Grandma Dearman (otherwise known simply as Maw-Maw) making Tea Cakes for my sisters and me while living in Louisiana. We loved eating them piping hot right out of her oven. A few years later our family moved to Memphis leaving behind Maw-Maw, along with many aunts, uncles and cousins. Our sweet grandmother would make these Tea Cakes and package them in a wax paper lined box and send them via the Post Office straight up to Tennessee. The postal service wasn't real swift back in those days and the cakes were a little stale by the time we got them. However, we didn't care how fresh they "weren't" because it was truly love in a box from her. My grandmother didn't really have time to single out any of her grandchildren and do many special things with them one on one because she had well over 30 grandkids! So as we excitedly opened up that wax paper lined box we would smile, feeling special all the while.

Maw-Maw's Tea Cakes

2 cups flour
1 tablespoon baking powder
1 teaspoon salt
1/2 cup butter, softened
1 cup sugar
1 teaspoon vanilla extract
1 egg
1/2 cup buttermilk
1/8 cup sugar

Preheat oven to 350 degrees.

Prepare two baking sheets with cooking spray or line with parchment paper and set aside.

In a medium bowl combine the flour, baking powder and salt. With a fork or a whisk stir to combine and set aside.

In the bowl of an electric mixer cream together the butter, sugar and vanilla extract. Beat in the egg. Add the buttermilk and beat on medium low until well combined.

Slowly add the dry ingredients and stir until you have soft dough and all of the dry ingredients are incorporated into the dough.

Turn the dough out onto a floured surface and gently knead about 3 to 4 times. Do not over work the dough as it will become dense and tough. Roll the dough out with a floured rolling pin to about 1/2 inch thick. Cut with a 2 1/2 inch biscuit cutter and place on the prepared cookie sheets.

Bake for about 15 minutes or until they are very light golden in color. Watch the cakes carefully since they are thin and some brown quicker than others. Sprinkle with sugar while they are still hot.

Let the cakes rest on the cookie sheet for 3 minutes. Gently transfer to a baking rack to cool.

Yield: 1 1/2 dozen

Rum, Raisin and Coconut Rice Pudding

1/3 cup raisins
1 tablespoon dark rum
1/4 cup hot water
1 cup coconut flakes, divided
2 cups water
1 teaspoon salt
1 cup uncooked white rice
zest of 1 lime, divided
juice of 1 lime
1 cinnamon stick, 3 inches long
3 1/2 cups whole milk
3 egg yolks, lightly whipped
3/4 cup sugar
ground cinnamon

Preheat oven to 350 degrees.

In a small dish combine the raisins, rum and hot water; mix together and set aside.

Place the coconut flakes on a foil lined baking sheet and place in the preheated oven. Bake for 5 minutes or until lightly golden brown. Watch carefully as it will brown quickly. Remove from the oven and set aside.

In a small saucepan with a tight fitting lid add the water, salt, rice, 1 teaspoon of the lime zest, juice of 1 lime and cinnamon stick; bring to a boil over medium high heat. Once the water is boiling turn the heat to a very low simmer and place a tight fitting lid over the saucepan. Cover and cook for 20 minutes. Do not lift the lid! After 20 minutes remove from heat and set aside for 5 minutes. After 5 minutes lift the lid, remove cinnamon stick and fluff rice with a fork.

Meanwhile in a separate sauce pan add the milk, egg yolks, sugar and raisin mixture; whisk to combine well. Cook for 20 minutes over medium to medium high heat while stirring constantly otherwise it will scald on the bottom. Continue to cook until the mixture starts to thicken, about 20 minutes. Once it has thickened enough to cling to a spoon add 1/2 cup of the toasted coconut. Stir in enough rice until you have a thick pudding.

Garnish with ground cinnamon, toasted coconut and lime zest.

Serve hot or cold.

Yield: Serves 6

For as long as I can remember our daughter Shelby has spent her summers making cobblers for the family, especially for her grandfather, Floyd. He loved cobblers! I don't remember ever seeing just one made at our house. It has always been two, one for us and one for Floyd. Blueberry season is a favorite of ours because we know that after we pick the blueberries and deliver them to Shelby she will undoubtedly take care of us!

Shelby's Cobbler

4 cups berries, apples, peaches or fruit of choice (if using apples add a little cinnamon to the sugar)
2 1/4 cups sugar, divided
2 cups flour
2 teaspoons baking powder
1/2 cup butter, melted
1 1/4 cups milk
1/2 gallon vanilla ice cream

Preheat oven to 350 degrees.

Prepare a 13x9x2 baking dish with cooking spray and set it aside.

Wash the fruit and slice it if necessary. Place the fruit in a large bowl and sweeten it with 1/4 cup of the sugar. Stir the fruit gently and set it aside. In a large bowl mix together the flour, baking powder and 2 cups of sugar; combine well. Add the melted butter and milk, mix on low to medium low speed with an electric mixer. Do not over mix the batter as it will get tough. Pour the batter into the prepared baking dish. Place the sweetened fruit on top of the batter.

Bake for 1 hour and 15 minutes or until it is golden brown and bubbly in the center. Remove from the oven and let it cool. It can be served warm or at room temperature. It's always better with a scoop of ice cream!

Note: Do not overfill the baking dish. I also suggest placing a foil lined baking sheet under the baking dish in order to catch any over flow.

Yield: Serves 6 to 8

Apple Ring Treats

This was one of our favorite after school snacks! We would rush home from school, make this treat and eat it while watching "Leave it to Beaver", "The Brady Bunch", "Mayberry RFD" and of course "I Love Lucy". What fond memories!

Ingredients are for one person. Double for two, triple for three, etc.

1/4 teaspoon cinnamon
1 tablespoon sugar
1 slice country white bread
2 tablespoons peanut butter
2 candied apple rings

Turn oven to broil. Line a cookie sheet with aluminum foil.

Combine the cinnamon and sugar in a small bowl and set aside. Spread peanut butter on one side of the bread. Place 2 candied apple rings on top of the peanut butter. Sprinkle the cinnamon and sugar combination over the bread, peanut butter and candied apple rings. Place on the foil lined cookie sheet and broil in oven until crust of bread is golden brown and peanut butter is gooey! Watch very carefully as it browns quickly.

Yield: Serves 1

Brian's Banana Cake

I made this cake for some very dear friends in the fall of 1991. It was a very cold autumn day and everyone was a bit chilly, not to mention that their son Brian was a very hungry 15 year old. While we sat talking and warming up in front of the fireplace with our coffee, hot chocolate and cake it was obvious how much Brian loved this treat. I made this cake for him many times over the years and I don't think I ever could again without thinking of him.

Cake:
1/2 cup butter, softened
1 cup sugar
2 eggs
1 cup banana, mashed
1/4 cup milk
1/4 cup Jack Daniels Whiskey
2 1/4 cups flour
2 teaspoons baking powder
1/4 teaspoon baking soda
1/2 teaspoon salt

Frosting:
4 tablespoons butter, softened
1 ripe banana, mashed
3 cups confectioners' sugar
1 tablespoon Jack Daniels Whiskey

Cake:

Preheat oven to 350 degrees. Prepare two 9 inch cake pans with cooking spray and set aside.

With an electric mixer, cream butter in a medium size bowl. Slowly add sugar, beating until light and fluffy. Add the eggs one at a time, beating after each. Add the mashed banana, milk and Jack Daniels to cream mixture; beat well. Combine flour, baking powder, baking soda and salt in a separate bowl and whisk to combine. Add the dry ingredients to the wet mixture and stir, finish by beating for 3 minutes.

Pour evenly into the prepared cake pans. Bake for 30 minutes or until wooden toothpick inserted into the center comes out clean. Cool in pan for 10 minutes. Gently remove from pan and cool completely on wire racks.

Frosting:

Cream butter and banana together. Slowly add the sugar one large tablespoon at a time until it is all incorporated. Add the Jack Daniels and whip until it is completely combined. Spread over cooled cake.

Yield: Serves 8 to 10

Buttercream Frosting

1 cup butter, softened
4 cups confectioners' sugar
1 teaspoon vanilla extract
6 to 8 tablespoons milk

Add the butter to the bowl of an electric mixer and beat on medium speed until creamy. With mixer on low speed add one tablespoon of confectioners' sugar at a time until you have added all 4 cups. Blend until smooth. With mixer on medium speed add the vanilla extract and 6 to 8 tablespoons of milk. If you need a thicker frosting add more confectioners' sugar. If you need a thinner frosting add more milk one tablespoon at a time. Continue mixing for about 2 minutes.

This recipe makes enough to generously frost a double layer round cake.

Chewy Chocolate Brownies

3/4 cup butter, melted
1 3/4 cups sugar
2 tablespoons milk
2 eggs, beaten
2 teaspoons vanilla extract
1 1/3 cups flour
3/4 cup cocoa powder
1/2 teaspoon baking powder
1/4 teaspoon salt

Preheat oven to 350 degrees. Prepare a 13x 9x2 baking dish with cooking spray.

Melt the butter and set aside to cool to room temperature.

In a medium bowl combine the butter, sugar and milk. Stir in the eggs and vanilla extract. In a separate bowl whisk together the flour, cocoa powder, baking powder and salt. Stir the dry ingredients into the sugar and butter mixture; combine well. Spread evenly into the baking dish.

Bake for 20 to 25 minutes or until a wooden toothpick inserted in center comes out slightly sticky. Cool completely in baking dish on a wire rack. Cut into squares.

Yield: Serves 10 to 12

Chocolate Cake

This is definitely a family favorite! If there is mention of chocolate cake in our house it is assumed that this is the one! It is decadently good and rich!

Cake:
2 cups flour
1 1/2 cups sugar
1 teaspoon baking soda
1/2 teaspoon salt
1 cup butter
1 cup water
1/4 cup cocoa powder
2 eggs
3/4 cup sour cream

Frosting:
1/2 cup butter
1/4 cup cocoa powder
6 tablespoons milk
1 cup confectioners' sugar
1 teaspoon vanilla extract

Cake:
Preheat oven to 325 degrees. Prepare a 13x9x2 baking dish and set aside.

In a medium size mixing bowl combine the flour, sugar, baking soda and salt; combine and set aside. In a medium size saucepan bring butter, water and cocoa powder to a gentle boil, stir to combine and remove from heat. Let cool to room temperature. Pour cocoa mixture into a medium size mixing bowl and slowly add the dry ingredients a little at a time; mix well, scraping sides often. Add eggs and sour cream; beat for 2 to 3 minutes. Pour into the prepared baking dish.

Bake for 25 to 35 minutes or until a wooden toothpick inserted into center comes out clean. Place on wire cooling rack and let cool completely.

Frosting:
Over medium heat bring the butter, cocoa and milk to a simmer in a medium saucepan; while stirring constantly. Add the sugar one spoonful at a time to the cocoa mixture; stirring constantly. Once the sugar is dissolved completely add the vanilla extract; blend well. Pour over the cake while the frosting is hot.

Yield: Serves 12

Coconut Cream Pie

2/3 cup sugar
1/4 cup cornstarch
1/2 teaspoon salt
3 cups whole milk
3 eggs, separated (reserving yolks and whites)
1 cup coconut flakes, divided
1 teaspoon vanilla extract
9 inch pie shell, blind baked (see note)
6 tablespoons sugar

Preheat oven to 425 degrees.

Off heat combine sugar, cornstarch and salt in top of double boiler; mix well. Gradually add milk, while stirring. Cook over boiling water, stirring constantly, until mixture is thick enough to mound when dropped from a spoon. Cover and cook 10 minutes more over low heat, stirring occasionally. Let cool until lukewarm.

Beat egg yolks slightly. Stir a small amount of warm mixture into egg yolks, stirring constantly. Immediately pour egg yolk mixture back into remaining warm mixture, blending well. Cook 2 minutes more, stirring constantly. Remove from heat. Gently stir in 3/4 cup coconut and vanilla extract. Pour into baked pie shell. Let cool completely.

To make the meringue, beat egg whites in bowl until foamy, using an electric mixture at high speed. Gradually add 6 tablespoons of sugar, 1 tablespoon at a time, beating well after each addition. Continue beating until stiff, glossy peaks form when beaters are slowly lifted.

Gently spread meringue over custard filling starting around edges, mounding in the center and pushing back out to the edges. Sprinkle with 1/4 cup of coconut.

Bake in preheated oven for 5 minutes or until meringue is lightly browned. Cool on rack before serving. Once completely cooled the pie may be stored in refrigerator.

Note: To blind bake a pie shell-If the pie shell is to be baked without a filling, prick the bottom and sides all over with a fork. Be sure the holes are made all the way through so that the steam can escape during the baking to prevent the crust from puffing up. Don't prick pie shell if the filling is to be baked in it.

Yield: Serves 6 to 8

Coconut Topped Cupcakes

This is a summer time favorite. I have witnessed first hand this recipe converting non-coconut loving people to coconut lovers!

Cupcakes:
1/2 cup butter (room temperature)
1 cup sugar
2 large eggs
3/4 teaspoon vanilla extract
1 1/2 cups flour
1/2 teaspoon baking powder
1/2 cup whole milk

Frosting:
1/2 cup butter (room temperature)
1/2 cup cream cheese (room temperature)
1 cup confectioners' sugar
2 teaspoons coconut extract
2 cups coconut flakes

Cupcakes:
Preheat oven to 350 degrees. Line a 12 cup muffin tin with paper liners.

With an electric mixer on medium speed, beat the butter and sugar until pale and fluffy. Beat in the eggs one at a time and add the vanilla extract. Reduce speed; beat in the flour, baking powder and milk.

Spoon the mixture evenly into the paper liners. Bake for 15 to 17 minutes or until a wooden toothpick inserted into the center of one of the cupcakes comes out clean. Cool on wire baking rack. Do not frost until completely cool.

Frosting:
Beat butter and cream cheese together until smooth and creamy. Continue to beat while adding 1 tablespoon of confectioners' sugar at a time until well incorporated. Add coconut extract and continue to beat until fluffy. Frost cupcakes and sprinkle with coconut.

Yield: Makes 12 cupcakes

Coffee and Toffee Ice Cream

2 teaspoons instant coffee
1/2 cup boiling water
12 graham crackers (2 cups crushed)
1/2 cup butter, melted
1 1/2 quarts vanilla ice cream, softened
6 Heath candy bars (1.4 ounces each), crushed into small pieces and divided
2 cups heavy whipping cream
2 tablespoons Creme De Cocoa

Combine the instant coffee and boiling water, stir and set aside.

Place the graham crackers in the bowl of a food processor and pulse until you have fine crumbs. Add the melted butter and combine with a fork until the crumbs are mixed well. Place the graham cracker crumbs and butter mixture into the bottom of a 9 inch round springform pan and pat down gently, covering the bottom evenly.

In a medium size mixing bowl combine the softened ice cream, coffee and 4 of the crushed Heath candy bars. Stir to combine.

Add ice cream mixture to the springform pan and garnish the top with the remaining crushed Heath bars. Cover with plastic wrap and freeze until solid.

Place a large mixing bowl and beaters in the freezer for at least 15 minutes before whipping the cream. Just before serving the ice cream add the whipping cream to the chilled mixing bowl. Whip until soft peaks form; adding the Creme De Cocoa about halfway through the process. Keep whipped cream cold in the refrigerator until ready to use.

Let the ice cream sit for 10 minutes at room temperature before serving. Release from springform pan and cut into 8 to10 slices

Place a dollop of whipping cream over the top of each ice cream serving and garnish with remaining pieces of broken Heath Bars.

Yield: Serves 8 to 10

Creme Brulee

1 egg
4 egg yolks
1/4 cup sugar
3 tablespoons vanilla extract
2 1/2 cups heavy cream
1/2 cup sugar

Preheat oven to 300 degrees. Prepare a 10 x10 inch baking dish or 6 individual ramekins with cooking spray and set aside.

In a bowl combine egg, egg yolks, sugar and vanilla extract. Beat lightly with a whisk until well combined. Add heavy cream and whisk until mixed thoroughly.

Pour into the baking dish or divide into individual ramekins.

Set the baking dish with the custard mixture into a larger shallow pan filled with water. The water should come about halfway up the baking dish.

Place in the oven for about 40 to 45 minutes or until set but still trembling. Set aside to cool and when it reaches room temperature place in the refrigerator for 6 hours or overnight.

Before serving, sprinkle with sugar and brown the top of the custard by setting it in a broiler or burning with a torch.

Note: If you are going to brown the top by placing it in a broiler bring the custard to room temperature first.

Yield: Serves 6

Frozen Lime Pie

This recipe started as a craving when I was pregnant with our daughter Shelby. I taste tested every lime pie in the Cayman Islands until I found this recipe which was perfect to me. It's not too sweet or sour, nor does it have a Jello consistency. It is creamy, light and full of just the right amount of tartness. Thanks Shelby, I couldn't have done it without you!

Filling:
2 cans (14 ounces each) sweetened condensed milk
3 egg yolks
1 1/4 cups fresh lime juice
2 (9 inch) graham cracker pie crust
Meringue:
1 cup egg whites
1 cup sugar
zest of 1/2 lime

Filling:
Preheat oven to 300 degrees.

In the bowl of an electric mixer combine the milk, egg yolks and lime juice. Mix on medium low speed.

Divide mixture evenly between the two pie crust and bake for 8 minutes until just set.

Remove from the oven and set aside to cool completely.

Meringue:
Preheat oven to 350 degrees.

In the bowl of an electric mixer combine the egg whites and sugar; beat on high speed until stiff peaks form.

Spread the meringue on top of the pies by starting at the edges, mounding in the center and pushing back out to the edges. Bake for 5 minutes or until the meringue is lightly browned. Cool on a wire baking rack.

Freeze for at least 6 hours before serving. Garnish with lime zest.

Yield: Makes 2 pies

Oatmeal Cookies

2 cups flour
1/2 teaspoon baking powder
1 teaspoon baking soda
1/2 teaspoon salt
1/2 cup butter
1/2 cup vegetable oil
1 cup brown sugar
1 cup sugar
1 teaspoon vanilla extract
1 teaspoon cinnamon
2 eggs
3 cups quick cooking oats
1 cup of any of the following: chocolate chips, butterscotch chips, nuts, raisins or any combination of your choice

Preheat oven to 350 degrees.

In a medium bowl whisk together the flour, baking powder, baking soda and salt; set aside.

In a medium bowl cream together the butter, oil, brown sugar, sugar, vanilla extract and cinnamon until smooth. Beat in eggs one at a time. Gradually stir in the dry ingredients until well blended. Gently and a little at a time stir in the oats and chips.

Refrigerate dough for an hour before baking and in between batches to keep cool and thick.

Drop by rounded teaspoons onto an ungreased cookie sheet.

Bake for 10 to 12 minutes or until edges are golden. Let cookies cool for a few minutes before transferring to wire racks to cool completely.

Yield: Makes 3 dozen

Pumpkin Log

3 eggs
2/3 cup canned pumpkin
1 cup sugar
1 teaspoon baking soda
1/2 teaspoon cinnamon
3/4 cup flour
2 tablespoons walnuts, chopped (optional)
1 cup cream cheese
2 tablespoons butter, softened
3/4 teaspoon vanilla extract
1 1/4 cups powdered sugar

Preheat oven to 375 degrees.

Prepare a 9x13 inch cookie sheet with cooking spray and neatly line with parchment paper. Set aside.

In a medium size bowl beat the eggs and add the pumpkin, sugar, baking soda, cinnamon and flour; mix well. Pour ingredients onto the cookie sheet in a tidy rectangular shape. Sprinkle with chopped walnuts if desired. Bake for 15 minutes or until center comes out clean when you insert a toothpick.

Sprinkle 1/4 cup of the powdered sugar onto a clean kitchen cloth. Very gently turn the pumpkin cake onto the cloth while it is still hot and carefully roll into a long cylinder shape and let cool.

In a small bowl combine cream cheese, butter, vanilla extract and 3/4 cup of the powdered sugar. Unroll cake and spread filling on top. Roll again like a jelly roll.

Cool and place on a serving platter and sprinkle with the remaining 1/4 cup of the powdered sugar. Slice into 8 pieces and serve.

Yield: Serves 8

Southern Banana Pudding

1 box (11 ounces) vanilla wafer cookies
4 cups whole milk
2 boxes vanilla pudding, cook and serve, not instant
4 bananas, sliced 1/4 inch thick

Line the bottom and sides of a 2 quart glass trifle bowl or deep serving bowl with the vanilla wafers and set aside.

In a large saucepan over medium heat add the milk. Slowly add the pudding mix while whisking constantly. Watch carefully as it will burn on the bottom very easily. Bring the mixture to a low boil and continue to stir constantly until the pudding has thickened. Once it has thickened remove from heat.

In the wafer lined bowl layer in the ingredients while the pudding is still warm. Alternately layer in the pudding, bananas and more wafers. Finishing with wafers garnishing the top of the pudding.

Set aside to cool and refrigerate or serve warm. I particularly like my banana pudding really cold. This is the perfect dessert to make the day before serving.

Yield: Serves 8

Coconut Chocolate Fondue

1/2 cup butter
1/2 cup cocoa powder
1/4 cup sugar
1/3 cup Coco Lopez (cream of coconut)
1/2 cup heavy cream
1 teaspoon coconut extract
Assorted Fondue Dippers: angel food cake cubes, pound cake cubes, marshmallows, cherries, grapes, oranges segments, pineapple chunks, strawberries or apple slices

Melt the butter in a small saucepan over low heat. Remove the saucepan from the heat and immediately stir in the cocoa powder. Add the sugar, Coco Lopez and cream. Cook over low heat while stirring constantly until the mixture is smooth and hot. Remove from heat and stir in the coconut extract. The fondue will thicken slightly as it cools. Serve warm with assorted fondue dippers as listed above. This recipe makes about 1 1/2 cups of fondue.

Yield: Serves 8 to 10

Pecan Pie

1 cup sugar
1/2 cup corn syrup
1/4 cup margarine, melted
3 eggs, well beaten
1 cup pecans, halved
1 unbaked pie shell

Preheat oven to 350 degrees.

Combine sugar, syrup and margarine in a medium bowl; beat until well blended. Add beaten eggs and mix thoroughly. Stir in the pecans and pour into the unbaked pie crust. Bake for 40 to 45 minutes or until pie is set. Serve cold or at room temperature.

Yield: Serves 8

Carrot Cake

Cake:
2 tablespoons butter, room temperature
1 3/4 cups sugar
1 cup vegetable oil
4 eggs
2 cups flour, plus additional to prepare pans
2 teaspoons baking powder
2 teaspoons baking soda
1 teaspoon salt
2 teaspoons cinnamon
3 cups carrots, grated
1/3 cup Jack Daniels Whiskey
1/2 cup pecans, chopped

Frosting:
1 can (16 ounces) crushed pineapple, drained while reserving 3 tablespoons of juice
1 cup butter, room temperature
2 cups cream cheese, room temperature
4 teaspoons vanilla extract
4 cups confectioners' sugar

Cake:
Preheat oven to 350 degrees. Grease the bottom and sides of 3 (9 inch) cake pans with butter; cover the bottoms with a circle of wax or parchment paper, butter the paper and sift flour over the pans; invert and tap to remove excess flour.

Using an electric mixer cream sugar and oil together until smooth. Beat in the eggs one at a time. In a separate mixing bowl combine the dry ingredients; flour, baking powder, baking soda, salt and cinnamon, whisking to combine. By spoonfuls slowly add the dry ingredients to the cream mixture while mixing on low to medium low speed, scraping sides often. Only mix until everything is incorporated. Do not over mix. By hand gently fold in carrots, Jack Daniels Whiskey and pecans.

Pour batter into cake pans dividing evenly between the 3 pans. Bake until a toothpick inserted into the center of the cakes comes out clean, about 25 minutes. Let the cakes cool in the pans for 10 minutes, then gently invert onto a raised backing rack to finish cooling.

Frosting.
With an electric mixer on low to medium low speed make the frosting by creaming together the butter, cream cheese and vanilla extract. Slowly add the confectioners' sugar until you have a smooth mixture. Add the reserved pineapple juice and continue to mix until well combined.

Place a completely cooled layer of cake onto a cake platter. Spread that layer with 1/2 of the crushed pineapple. Add a layer of frosting. Place the second layer of cake on top of the first and spread the rest of the pineapple on that layer and add a layer of frosting. Place the third layer on top and frost the entire cake with remaining frosting.

Serve immediately or refrigerate. An hour before serving remove cake from refrigerator and bring to room temperature.

Serves 8 to 10

French Silk Pie

Although this is the last recipe in the book it should be the first because it is probably one of the best that I have ever acquired. Everyone loves, loves, loves this pie! It was given to me by our friend, John. He was kind enough to share and with his permission I "tweaked" it just a tad. It really didn't need changing but our family likes a little less sugar and a bit more chocolate. The meringue crust is so light but yet it can easily support the richness of the filling. John advised me right from the get go to make two pies if I was going to make one because it will be gone quickly. He was absolutely right, therefore I highly suggest you double the recipe. One summer when I made this delicious treat a couple of our neighbors were fighting over the last piece. We will just say that the negotiations heated up and the stakes went pretty high until they finally came to a mutually beneficial compromise. In the end they were both able to enjoy the last of it together. Now, I'm not going to name names but you know who you are!

Thanks for sharing John!

Meringue Crust:
3 egg whites
1 pinch salt
1/4 teaspoon cream of tartar
1/2 teaspoon vanilla extract
1/2 cup sugar

Preheat oven to 275 degrees. Generously butter one 8" pie plate and set aside.

Over a small bowl, separate the egg yolks from the whites. Discard egg yolks. Combine egg whites, salt and cream of tartar in a large mixing bowl of an electric mixer. Start mixer on low and increase the speed to medium and then to high; beat until soft peaks form. Add the vanilla extract and slowly add the sugar, continue to beat for a few more minutes until the sugar is dissolved. At this point you should have stiff peaks. Be careful not to over mix.

Gently spread the meringue evenly into the prepared pie plate while covering the bottom and neatly spreading up the sides. Bake for one hour. Remove from oven and cool completely on a cooling rack.

Chocolate Filling:
1 cup butter, softened
1 cup sugar
2 ounces unsweetened chocolate squares
2 teaspoons vanilla extract
4 eggs

In a large mixing bowl of an electric mixer beat the softened butter until fluffy. Gradually add the sugar by tablespoons and beat until smooth; set aside.

Slowly and gently melt the chocolate squares in a double boiler (or a small heat safe bowl on top of a small saucepan) over simmering water until completely melted.

Add the chocolate and vanilla extract to the creamed butter and sugar mixture. Cool to room temperature. Beat the eggs in one at a time; beat on high for four minutes. The mixture should be light and fluffy. Refrigerate the filling until ready to assemble the pie.

Whipped Cream Topping:
2 cups heavy whipping cream
1 1/2 tablespoons confectioners' sugar
2 tablespoons Cream De Cocoa
1 chocolate candy bar (dark or milk chocolate)

Place your beaters and mixing bowl in the freezer for at least 15 minutes before whipping the cream. In the chilled mixing bowl add the heavy whipping cream and beat on medium high to high speed for about 5 minutes. Once the cream has formed soft peaks add the confectioners' sugar one spoonful at a time. Add the Cream De Cocoa. Beat a few minutes longer until the whipped cream has stiff peaks; do not over mix.

Assembling the Pie:
Place the chocolate filling into the cooled meringue crust and smooth out evenly. Add the whipped cream to the top of the filling and spread by starting at the edges and mounding toward the middle, then bringing back to the edges. Gently shave the chocolate candy bar over the top for garnish. Refrigerate until ready to serve.

Makes 1 pie

The End of The Road

Index